THE
COASTLINE
SERIES

SOLENT SHORES

John Glasspool

Illustrated by Jane Michaelis

NAUTICAL

© John Glasspool 1988

First published in Great Britain by
Nautical Books
an imprint of
A & C Black (Publishers) Ltd
35 Bedford Row, London, WC1R 4JH

Glasspool, John, 1932-
    Solent shores.—(Coastline series).
    1. England. Solent region. Visitors' guides
    I. Title   II. Series
    914.22'7

ISBN 0-7136-5740-5

Printed and bound in Great Britain

Contents

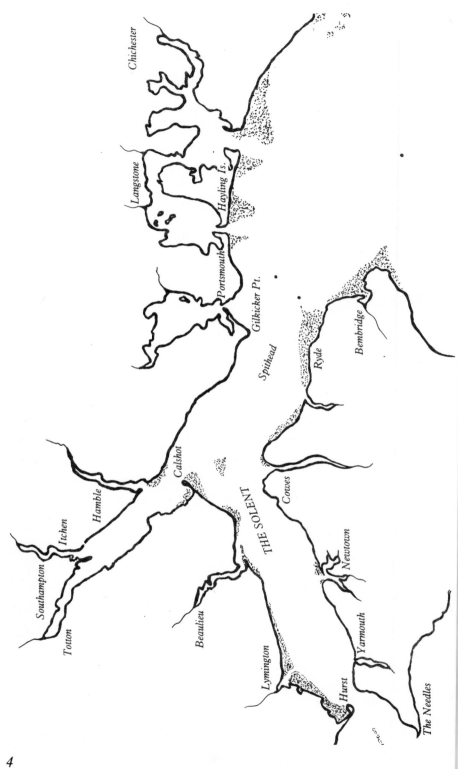

Chichester

Langstone

Hayling Is.

Portsmouth

Gilkicker Pt.

Spithead

Ryde

Bembridge

Southampton

Itchen

Hamble

Calshot

Cowes

Newtown

THE SOLENT

Totton

Beaulieu

Lymington

Yarmouth

Hurst

The Needles

Foreword

THIS is claimed to be neither a formal guidebook to the Solent shores, nor much less a pilot to its waters. Good reading about the Solent abounds and some of it is listed at the end of the book, with grateful thanks to those authors who have corrected this one's faulty memory about many details. I have assumed that the reader will derive fun from exploring this lovely area by water where possible, with hints on some things to look for beyond the immediate shoreline. It is based on the belief, formed from years of happy sailing on these waters, that the smaller the boat for the job the better. As for the absence of fine detail and failure to mention so many worthy things, I'll plead that this view of the Solent is meant to be more impressionist – although this is not offered as an excuse for inaccuracies – and is an attempt to capture something of the Solent's beauty and personality.

J. G.

I would like to thank the following for their help. Martin Woodward of Bembridge Maritime Museum, Nigel Overton of Southampton Maritime Museum and Chris Hammond of Hill Head.

Jane Michaelis

Approach

THE most vivid way to understand how the Solent and its collection of small estuaries owe their existence to the presence of the Isle of Wight is to approach in a small boat on a coastwise passage from east or west. From inside, looking at its gentle slopes across the gap of two or three miles that separate it from the Hampshire shore, it is easy to overlook what a mighty breakwater the Island is, protecting not only the waterways but the mainland countryside several miles inland of them. The northern face of the Island is gentle, a sort of continuation of Hampshire across the water. But from the Channel it presents a massive, almost overbearing appearance which, in contrast to the flat lands of the coastal plains of Hampshire and West Sussex, dominates the view from a boat for miles. On a coastal passage from eastward, for example, from the East Anglian harbours or the Thames Estuary, a sailor will have followed the chalk cliffs round from the North Foreland and past Folkestone to the sudden flat contrast of Romney Marsh and Pevensey Levels. The chalk rears dramatically again at Beachy Head, from which the line of the South Downs recedes inland to the west, leaving the shore for the next 50 miles or so flat and (to seamen) comfortless, pierced by a couple of river-estuary harbours of uninviting access, and which call for good pilotage and a pressing reason to make them in breezy conditions. Selsey Bill slinks out to seaward, flat and treacherous as a coral reef, with some choice horrors to seaward of it in the hills and dells of the sunken landscape of the Owers, through the contorted seabed of which the tides seethe with awesome power.

By then, heaving up massive on the western skyline, there is the Island. Approaching it in the latter part of the day, when the great Downs are in shadow, the sailor sees the chalky glint of the Foreland, like the head of a giant serpent, pointing straight at him. The dark line of the Downs, running down the east–west axis of the Island, strengthen the image: the serpent has hunched shoulders. To the left and southern end of this mass there are higher hills which swoop down to the sea with the dramatic suddenness of mountains beside a Scottish loch.

The small boat stands on, picking up the first of the buoys that guide her past the great spread of Horse Sand on the starboard hand, with her crew probably enjoying their first view of the fabled seascape and a break in the long passage down-Channel, for nobody ever sails past the Solent without stopping. Away to port is the dark, deceptively rickety looking structure of the Nab Tower, the main big-ship mark for this eastern approach, with its famous slight tilt. A cluster of satellite buoys mark the tight turn through the New Grounds towards the red Warner buoy with its urgent, quick-flashing light. Then, the squat shapes of the No Man's Land and Horse Sand Forts mark the true gateway from the open Channel into the Solent. And by the time the sailor can spare a look around at the scenery from his pilotage, he discovers that the Island shore has quite changed.

The frowning seaward face has been transformed into gentle grassland, trees and villas, with Ryde rising up to the skyline and its famous church spire. To the west of the resort and its enormous expanse of sand the trees advance right down to the low-lying shore, which has become gentle and of a comfortingly small scale. On the mainland side, blue in the distance, the South Downs, launched in such fine style from Beachy, march away to the northwest. To the west of Southampton Water, the great breach in the mainland shoreline ahead, are the dark tree-clad miles of the New Forest.

From the west, the sequence is similar in several ways. From Portland to Anvil Point the beautiful Dorset coast offers no shelter after Weymouth: Lulworth Cove, a magical place to visit in fair weather, is certainly no harbour of refuge. By the time Poole Bay opens on the port hand and the unpleasant tide rips of the Dorset headlands (an interesting counterpart to those off Selsey) have been passed, there again, projecting from the Island, is that mountainous mass, enormous and more chalky at this end, giving an even more vivid sense of being stared down at by the sharp-beaked serpent's head of the Needles.

Of the two approaches, this is the trickier and a skipper needs to be sure of his tides. No sailing vessel can hope to make much against the stream that sluices through Hurst Narrows on the ebb, and a fair breeze strong enough to encourage him to try, would be rearing up seas of remarkable steepness on the weather-going stream.

All that, and a very narrow channel in which to work, with various rocky hazards on the Island side and the unfriendly roar of the grating pebbles on the Shingles Bank on the other, makes the passage of the

Needles Channel something to try for the first time in good, clear conditions. This entrance is the narrowest part of the Solent, and its most dangerous. On the mainland side Hurst Spit, a long shingle bank that is a small version of the great Chesil Beach at Portland complete with lighthouses and a castle at its seaward end, closes the gap to about half a mile, through which the tide has to jostle and squeeze on the ebb. Here too, and perhaps because of those strong streams, is the deepest part as well, getting on for 200 feet deep in that narrow bottleneck, compared with less than half that depth for most of the eastward approach. But once the Hurst hazards are passed, and with more dramatic suddenness than in the arrival at the eastern end, the open-sea urgency drops behind; the crumbly, craggy cliffs on the Island side recede into the background, giving way to gentle woods and pastoral landscape levelling down to the banks of the western River Yar and the little town of Yarmouth beyond.

After the raw newness of the Needles rocks and its associated chalk precipice of Scratchells Bay, this sheltered landscape looks gentle and comfortably old. The Needles are, in fact, very new in geological terms.

The Solent as we know it today would rate as no age at all, although the slow processes that laid down its ingredients took a timescale hard to comprehend. A deep sea covered everything for millions of years, long enough for the microscopic skeletons of countless billions of planktonic organisms to settle on the bed of that sea, eventually forming a deposit 1,500 feet thick, the weather-shaped remains of which are now the chalk downs of Hampshire and the Isle of Wight. Within the last million years the one-time seabed slowly lifted and southern England was joined to France and other now submerged lands. Other inundations laid down the sands, sediments and clays which provide the characteristic varied texture of the Solent shores today. Before the last Ice Age the chalk ran unbroken from the Needles across what is now Poole Bay to Old Harry Rocks on the Purbeck coast of Dorset. The raw, broken edges of both indicate that in geological age their sundering is quite new.

After the last Ice Age, with the melting of the massive ice cap over the northern hemisphere, the sea level rose swiftly and broke through that rampart of chalk into the low-lying land beyond, where Christchurch and Poole Bays are now. Before the breach the Solent River ran towards the east from its twin headwaters, the rivers Piddle and Frome in Dorset. It flowed from what is now Poole Harbour, picking up other tributaries, the Avon and Stour, Test, Itchen, the Meon and smaller streams, until it joined the sea somewhere well south of Selsey Bill. Off Selsey, among the vast area of contorted seabed that extends southward to the Owers, lie the pickled remains of tree stumps. What we are left with, then, from this succession of drownings, uprisings, deposition, erosion and other processes which must have been quite unpleasant, had anybody been around, is an area of beautiful marine countryside, sheltered from the hard sea winds by the Island Downs to the south, and by the South Downs of the mainland from the worst of northerly weather. The gravels make stable banks for the clear streams that spring from the chalk, and the sediments have given the area a fertile mantle of soil. As the rivers approached the main water they slowed, allowing the growth of reedy marsh that provided a rich habitat for wildlife. By the time man arrived to exploit it all, there was good access by water inland, plenty of timber, flints and chalk for building, reeds for thatching, game to be hunted and, eventually, good soil for pasture and agriculture. No wonder the lands around the Solent were so popular with migrants and invaders from mainland Europe seeking a convenient and benign bridgehead. The Germanic tribes in particular thought highly of it, leaving us placenames such as Hayling, Wymering (part of Portsmouth) and Eling, the tiny port at the head of Southampton Water. They were the first really sea-minded people to realise the Solent's possibilities and began the thousand year history of settlement after Roman times in which the area came to take centre-stage position on England's maritime scene.

It is the variety of scenery in a small compass, along with the extra fascination that any water brings to a landscape, that creates the magic of the place. In our overcrowded age, we look for relaxation, for undeveloped places, for peace and solitude with the same care as the old North Germans sought out land with possibilities for settlement. Here again, the Solent comes up trumps.

Along the Island shore, from the western fringe of Cowes to Newtown Creek and beyond, there are miles of coast which are so satisfying to sail past because they are virtually free of buildings. This stretch of shore remains almost the same as people would have known it centuries ago, thanks not to some conscious conservation effort to keep it that way, but to a happy geological accident, unpopular to would-be developers but a blessing to those who appreciate a bit of coastline that has escaped them. All these low cliffs and bluffs are crumbly. The Blue Slipper clay, sticky putty-like lumps of which cling to the boots of walkers along the north shore, is too unstable to allow building. So this precious few miles has been spared the rows of bungalow windows staring seaward which has ruined other places. The woodlands and farm pastures run to the cliff edge. There are one or two holiday camps too, but so discreetly sited well back from the coast that you can easily pretend there's hardly a soul for miles. What is more, the beaches below these crumbly cliffs, where the Blue Slipper mixes with coarse gravel, dead saplings which have broken away from the bluffs above and the seaweedy ledges offshore, make this stretch an uncongenial place for people used to more comfortable seaside amenities. So except for beach fishermen and walkers, the shore stays fascinatingly deserted.

On the north side there is a similar appearance of undisturbed nature.

Westward from Lepe, which is a popular seaside spot for Southampton and Waterside people, there is hardly any public access to the sea all the way to Lymington. Again, the shore is not the stuff of which resorts are made; a broad band of saltmarsh cuts off the foreshore from the open water. So again, very few people, and a largely undisturbed paradise for seabirds, wild flowers which thrive on a salty habitat, and when looking at the landscape from boats, the happy illusion that, despite the chimneys of Fawley Refinery lurking on the right-hand edge of the view, the New Forest begins almost at the water's edge and runs uninterrupted inland for miles.

Old Harry Rocks

1 Bembridge to Cowes

BEMBRIDGE Harbour or, to give it its older name, Brading Haven, is the only harbour on the Island that does not open due northward into the Solent. It lies half removed from the Solent proper and opens northeast towards the waters of St Helen's Roads and Spithead, and the great curve of Bracklesham Bay over on the mainland side. The seafront buildings at Southsea gleam like a little Miami on a clear day six miles away, not all that much farther than from Ryde. Until just over a century ago the harbour extended westward inland in a great tidal lagoon, but it was confined to its present area in the 1870s when a causeway dyke, the second and successful attempt to build one, cut off several hundred acres from the sea and made the ancient port of Brading an inland village. To seaward lie the rocky formations known collectively as the Bembridge Ledges, avoided with great respect by passing craft and providing something of a natural breakwater to protect the entrance from big Channel seas in easterly weather. The Downs around Brading give protection from the west and southwest.

Bembridge is an attractive and comfortable port for yachts and, like Yarmouth at the western end of the Island, is a useful setting-off point for boats waiting for an ease in the weather before a Channel crossing. Because of its narrow entrance, which virtually dries at low water, it is not to be relied on as a harbour of refuge. More accessible boltholes lie beyond the Spithead forts not far away. Brading – the Kinge's Towne of Bradynge – lies a mile or so to the west of the once-important port and is now a pleasant inland village. Bembridge itself is more modern, but with lots of seafaring associations particularly with the smugglers for whom it was once a favourite haunt.

Bembridge

From the foot of Brading on its hill, the eastern River Yar flows across marshy, low-lying land which gives an idea of the size of area covered by seawater at high tide before it was dyked. The Eastern Yar then nearly cut off the eastern tip of the Island, as the Western Yar nearly does between Freshwater and Yarmouth today.

With an eye to bringing those oozy acres into lucrative cultivation, Sir Bevis Thelwell, a courtier of King James I, enlisted Sir Hugh Myddleton, a goldsmith and engineer, to build a dyke at the eastern end. They hired Dutch labour and managed to isolate 700 acres of tidal mudland behind a wall of clay and stones. But after only a few years, the sea began to trickle through in 1630 and in the space of a few days a gap was eroded in the bank through which the water reclaimed the land. The tides came and went unhindered for nearly 250 years until in 1878 Jabez Balfour, a live-wire business entrepreneur, had the idea of developing Bembridge as a terminal for his proposed train-ferry service from Hayling Island. He formed a company to build a new dyke which was to be the embankment for his railway. After much difficulty and colossal expense which eventually ruined him, Balfour actually got his train-ferry scheme to run, but by 1886 it was taken over by the London, Brighton & South Coast Railway, which ceased operations two years later. But the company he formed, the Bembridge Harbour Improvement Company, is still in existence and among the ways it has lived up to its title was the creation of a new marina at the eastern end of the present harbour.

In the 18th and early 19th century the position of the harbour, discreetly hidden from the Solent despite the zealous watch kept by the Preventive men, was a thriving smuggling port. As late as 1836, when the heyday of smuggling was nearly over, a Coastguard report estimated that 10,000 barrels of spirit were getting ashore each year. Because the bulk prices were low, it enabled re-export across the Solent to mainland markets at a good profit. Today we find it hard not to have affection for smugglers, partly as rebels against oppressive officialdom but also as fine seamen.

One such was a local man called Dicky Dawes, or Daw, remembered to this day in the names Daw Bank and Daw Passage through the rocks of Bembridge Ledge. But Dicky was not the only member of his family to be notorious. He had a sister called Sophie, a good-looking lass by all accounts, who quite turned the head of a French aristocrat while plying her trade as a shellfish gatherer from the rocks at low tide, with her skirts hitched up to expose a fine pair of legs. The nobleman, the Baron de Feucheres, married her and took her off to France. The dark rumour is that she murdered him and returned to England where she lived in style until her death in 1840.

Just to the north of the harbour mouth, and of the fort which stands a little way offshore and makes a useful approach mark to help visiting sailors, is St Helen's Roads, for centuries a favourite anchorage for merchant vessels and men-of-war awaiting a favourable slant for setting off down-Channel. The oft-told tale is that the Royal Navy's love of smartness, maybe stimulated by this idle waiting, led to decks being buffed to alabaster brightness. Flat stones were ideal for this job, and the old churchyard at St Helen's is reputed to have donated a few, hence the name of the morning ritual, holystoning, the purpose of which is not only to improve the looks of a wooden deck, but to keep it free of any dangerously slippery film which might form.

On a blunt headland, just where the coast trends west towards Ryde, stands Seaview, a place which still manages to preserve its identity from the spread of the big resort around the corner. A building overlooking the shore is the home of the Seaview Yacht Club, founded in 1896 and around which, John Scott Hughes wrote 60 years later, 'so much of the life of the place is centred'. Seaview YC deserves special honour from dinghy sailing people for its particular interest in their branch of boating. This led, a little over 50 years ago, to one of the Solent's most popular and enduring small-boat classes, which doesn't merely survive today – it flourishes. In 1898, after a couple of years in which club meetings took place in various spare rooms in Seaview, it moved to its elegant clifftop headquarters. One of the early members was Percy Tatchell, who deserves to be better remembered for his life-long work to advance the cause of simple, practical boating and dinghy sailing. The lines of new designs by him appeared regularly in the yachting magazines over the years, based on the conviction that the fun to be had from a boat was not in relation to her size. One of his individualities was his advocacy of the facing-forward rowing position. He called it 'push rowing', and a feature of his design drawings was a sketched leg in the rowing position to assure his builders that he had not made a mistake in putting the stretchers and rowlock positions back to front. Early on, Percy

Seaview

Tatchell helped to organise Seaview YC's first handicap dinghy races back in 1904. The system worked well until Major Gordon Fowler and Lieutenant Commander Norman Ohlenschlager were the prime movers in establishing a small one-design for Seaview, small enough to be within a popular price range yet game enough to cope with the sea conditions off the club. George Feltham, whose yard used to be tucked in a corner of the Camber Docks at Portsmouth, was commissioned to produce a 12 foot clinker boat to the club specifications in 1930. And so the Sea View (two words) One-Design was launched, and the first of the class were sold at £26 – complete, in Feltham's specification, with anchor and bailer. From those modest beginnings flourished a class which was to become the most longlived and best supported in the Solent area, and in which many famous helmsmen first learned their skill. What is more remarkable, as Mr and Mrs B. G. Donald reveal in their history of the class, is that despite the almost universal takeover by fibreglass in boatbuilding, new boats are still being built for the class in the traditional way. At the last count, in the winter of 1986–7, the class numbered 115 boats, six new ones being built that winter, and with 95 being expected afloat for the following summer's racing programme.

Loyalty to the Sea View ODs has been helped by various rules, one of the strictest being that boats are not sold away out of the club, and others that govern the gear and fittings allowed. The boats bear the distinctive look of a George Feltham model; they are similar to the popular 12 foot Stormalongs he produced as a home class for Portsmouth Sailing Club, but with a lower freeboard. And the Sea View ODs managed to survive a mistake in the building of the first boats, whereby the bow mould had been placed farther aft than intended, making them rather fine forward. After the Second World War, when other builders were commissioned to produce dinghies for the class, the error was spotted from the original drawings and put right in later boats. Several of these tough little boats have made circumnavigations of the Isle of Wight.

Percy Tatchell would no doubt have been well pleased with such simple, practical craft. He went on designing small boats until the war. One of his last, a canoe-stern sailing and rowing boat, was featured in *Yachting World* magazine in May 1943 – designed for push rowing of course. Not long afterwards, as John Scott Hughes records, he made an enviable exit from this life, similar to that of the great Victorian singlehander Richard McMullen: he was found dead at the helm of one of his boats while sailing in the Solent.

Larger classes from this corner of the Solent are famous too. Based in Bembridge Harbour are the Swans, a small fleet of clinker centreboarders built post-war by Alan Coombes. The elegant Bembridge Redwings, distinctive for the cherry red sails that inspire the name, are an updated design from the 1930s of an original produced by Camper & Nicholsons of Gosport in 1896. The early Redwings had an unusually liberal class rule which allowed any rig to owners' ideas so long as it conformed to the specified sail area. I owned one of these veterans, the kingplank of which had a row of plugged holes where previous members had indulged in shifting the mast position back and forth. Seaview YC fields an elegant keelboat class called the Mermaids, ballast keel racers to a design from the 1950s by Arthur Robb. The original Mermaids were drawn to club requirements in 1922, by Alfred Westmacott.

Round the corner at Nettlestone Point, the foreshore becomes broad and sandy and a small ribbon of open land separates Seaview from Ryde, which faces its rival, Southsea – they are the only two major seaside resorts on the Solent – across four miles of water. Ryde is built on a slope running inland, and from the upper end of its busy George and Union Streets there are stirring low-level aerial views of the long pier, with the Solent and the mainland shore beyond. The pier, which has to stride out a good half mile across the sands to reach water deep enough for the Portsmouth ferries to come alongside, is a rail terminal. Steam locomotives have gone from the Island, as has nearly all its track. Holiday passengers bound for Sandown and Shanklin now ride in rolling stock which must remind Londoners of home: they are units once used on London Transport's Underground system.

On top of the town is the most conspicuous landmark for sailors anywhere in the eastern Solent. This is the 180 foot tower and spire of St James's Church, completed in 1872 and considered one of the best works of its architect Sir Giles Gilbert Scott, in a Victorian version of Early English Decorated style.

In late Victorian and Edwardian times Ryde was a fashionable yachting centre of high repute; something as puzzling then as now, according to Frank Cowper. 'Why it was ever chosen,' he wrote in 1893, 'passes my comprehension', citing the exposed and shallow anchorage and the chance of a wetting getting to shore by dinghy. The sands may be Ryde's glory as a resort; they are a sandcastle builder's delight, but a sailor's bane. Craft would have to stand more than a mile offshore to clear them even if the pier

Ryde

and the defence barrier extending out to No Man's Land Fort were not in the way.

But Ryde had one advantage over Cowes farther west, where deep water comes right up to the foot of the Royal Yacht Squadron walls. At Ryde the long sea front enabled spectators to watch the racing more easily. The Royal Victoria Yacht Club had been founded in 1845 by a breakaway group from the Royal Yacht Squadron at Cowes, as a tribute to Queen Victoria's honour to the Isle of Wight 'in having chosen Osborne House for a marine palace'. Ryde, under the patronage of the Island by Victoria and Albert in their 'marine palace' a few miles to the west, became a fashionable watering place. Some seafront villas and other buildings reflect this high-class boom. But as its prestige declined among the well-to-do Plain-Jane Cowes recovered hers, so far as sailing people were concerned, and the Victorian hope of turning sailing into a spectator sport faded. At Cowes, the idea of landsmen wishing to follow the racing was for years treated with polite disdain. Cowes Front is a marvellous place to watch the passing Solent scene, but not for seeing more than the first mile or so of a race before the fleet disappeared round Egypt Point westward, or behind a screen of vessels anchored in Cowes Roads to the east.

But now, perhaps, big changes are afoot, thanks to the America's Cup races off Fremantle and the 12 Metre series that preceded them. Small, remote-controlled cameras mounted aft on competing yachts, clear of everybody, or cameras in helicopters (or for less wind disturbance, airships) have brought sailing into the whites-of-their-eyes close range which we have come to expect from coverage of other sports. Watching the action comfortably on a television screen instead of having to endure English August weather on a draughty promenade, might well boost the spectator rating of yachting several hundred per cent in a short time.

At the time of writing it seems that Ryde may be due for a revival as a yachting station. Early in 1987 there were discussions between a developer and the local council about the siting of a marina on the shore west of the pier, with a dredged channel through the sand, presumably.

The Royal Victoria survived gracefully the shift of the limelight back to Cowes, until in the early 1960s it combined with Wootton Creek Sailing Club and moved to a clubhouse at nearby Fishbourne at the mouth of Wootton Creek, where its helpful hospitality is one of the pleasures of visiting Wootton from the sea.

Wootton Creek, despite the pressures which have grown on it gradually over the years, remains a charming place. Scenically, it looks full of promise of gentle exploration right from the entrance, as the tree-lined banks curve away inland from the busy Pool close by the Royal Victoria clubhouse. Thanks to the Sealink ferries, the approach channel from the Solent is dredged and clearly marked by a series of massive wooden dolphins which guide the visitor clear of the off-lying Wootton Rocks west of the entrance. The worst of bad form at Fishbourne is to hinder the ferries, which are very large for such a small port of call.

Upstream from Fishbourne, a pleasant inland voyage awaits small boats or those of modest draft up to the tidal sluice at Wootton Bridge, a largish village astride the main Newport–Ryde road about a mile or so inland. Holiday villages and houseboats share the shores with some fine houses and grounds. People who live beside the creek have a reputation for being helpful to boat people. Some have private jetties to which, with luck, the proper courteous approach and the necessary respect for people's property, a visitor might be invited to tie alongside if there is no room in the crowded Pool.

Ship and boatbuilding was carried on along the shores of Wootton Creek in a big way until recent times. During the Second World War the Ranelagh yacht yard employed several hundred people turning out small dinghies, air-sea rescue vessels, pontoons and other craft for Service use. In the early 19th century Wootton's output in tonnage was said to be greater than that of Cowes. In 1824 the best known vessel to be built on the creek, the Earl of Yarborough's ship-rigged *Falcon*, 350 tons, went down the ways at List's yard. Following the fashion of the day she shipped 20 guns. In October 1827, with Lord Yarborough abroad and flying his flags as 'Admiral of the Isle of Wight' and Commodore of the Royal Yacht Squadron, she was employed as a despatch vessel at the Battle of Navarino in the eastern Mediterranean. After an accident which put an end to the Earl's seagoing days, he sold her to the trading firm of Jardine Matheson where she did lucrative work as an opium clipper in Far East waters. Her sailing qualities made her popular with crews manning her.

Beside the creek until a few weeks before the outbreak of the Second World War was the resting place of the real-life heroine (under another name) of what Eric Hiscock unequivocally called the best yachting story ever written, and there are many lifelong devotees of *The Riddle of the Sands* who would agree with that. In 1983 Maldwin Drummond published the result of immense painstaking research into the life story of the unprepossessing lifeboat conversion called *Vixen* which Erskine Childers had sailed to the Frisian Islands and the Baltic, a voyage which provided the accurate background for *The Riddle*, and ensured immortality for *Vixen*, better known as *Dulcibella*.

She was built for the RNLI as a lifeboat for the Kingsgate station, about two miles from Margate, where she went into commission in 1880. She was sold out of the service in 1889 to a Ramsgate boatbuilder who converted her to a yacht, including adding a false counter. After that famous voyage, Childers sailed her in the Solent for a time before parting with her. She changed hands once or twice until she was taken to Wootton in 1932 as the latest acquisition of the boatyard proprietor Claude 'Happy' Hapgood. Hapgood's affection for the heroine of *The Riddle* was not in doubt, but at Wootton there was no hope of a second lease of life (or third?) in store for her. Interest in the boat grew in the 1930s and several tries were made to get a fund for her preservation going, but these failed. By 1939, following Claude Hapgood's death, she was in a rundown state when an offer came from a boatyard at Lymington to give her a lay-up berth until her future could be decided. In August of that year she set off on her last voyage, down the Solent to the Lymington River, with the pumps going steadily to keep her afloat. There she lay through the war years at the Lymington Slipway yard, visited occasionally by devoted fans of Childers' tale and getting more and more decrepit, until in March 1948, after the yard had changed hands and the restoration project was becoming an increasingly lost cause, she was condemned as junk and burned. Her remains were used to fire the steam chest used for bending frames and planks for new yachts. It's a sad but cautionary tale which emphasises that a lot more than sentiment is required in the financially demanding business of restoring and preserving an old vessel.

From Wootton Creek westward to Cowes lies probably the most tranquil shoreline on the Solent. Hardly a building can be seen, and an abundance of trees clothe the slopes almost to the tideline, giving a rare sense of privacy and peace. In most weathers during the sailing season this stretch of coast is sheltered, and makes a delightful anchorage for a lunchtime stop or for a summer laze on deck. Hardly visible among the rich growth of trees is the mouth of King's Quay Creek. I hesitate to recommend this little paradise for a visit because the shores are private property and the creek bed is preserved by the Nature Conservancy Council as a wildlife haven. But a brief visit on the tide should cause no offence, so long as nobody lands, and certainly not with a dog; a quiet circuit and respectful withdrawal without disturbing anything is what King's Quay requires. The name was already established when Charles I passed this way in 1647. After his escape from Hampton Court he took refuge in Place House at Titchfield where, persuaded that the Isle of Wight would be a safe haven, he rode to the shore near the tiny estuary of Titchfield Haven, where the Meon flows into the Solent, and embarked in a boat for the Island. It was at King's Quay where, by tradition, he landed. The original King of the Quay was, according to tradition, King John, who crossed over to nurse his political wounds after signing the Magna Carta. If the royal associations are doubtful, then so is the Quay of the name: today there isn't one. But no creek as handy as this would have been without traffic of some sort, before the days of metalled roads, and there is indication that King's Quay Creek was a small commercial port. Today it is silted up, which means that a visit by sailing dinghy is not only the most practical but the most appropriate way to get a glimpse of this magic place.

Between Ryde and Fishbourne a mass of russet and fine brickwork rises above the shoreline trees to mark Quarr Abbey. This was built in 1908–14

King's Quay

and is rated as the finest ecclesiastical building of brick in Europe. The association of an abbey with the site began in 1131, during the lordship of the island of Baldwin de Redvers. An ancient quarry nearby gave the place its name. The abbey, then of the Cistercian order, was the daughter house of Savigny in Normandy. It became the most important monastery on the Island and owned considerable property, even its own fleet of ships.

After his death in 1156 Baldwin de Redvers was buried in the abbey, followed in due time by his wife and young son. Quarr, like most monasteries, grew in power until the chill wind of the Dissolution. It was closed in July 1536 and sold to Southampton merchants who plundered the place so thoroughly that all the stone was removed. Some of it was used for Henry VIII's castles at East and West Cowes. Some of the monks crossed the Solent to Beaulieu, but their refuge there was not to be long before it too received the attention of Henry's men.

By an ironic twist of history, it was another spell of secular persecution, in France, that led to the abbey's rebirth. French Benedictine monks from Solesmes came to the Island in 1901 to get away from the uncongenial climate created by the anti-clerical government of the time. Among them was Dom Paul Bellot who had been trained as an architect. He designed the new building, combining byzantine pinnacled towers with patterned brick surfaces. Belgian bricks were used for the work, laid by Island workmen under Dom Paul's supervision. Today it is the most distinctive building on the Island, and the brown-red brickwork blends effectively with the trees that partially screen it from the shore. It is set in mature grounds which establish its modern role as an oasis of peace and a chance to put the distractions of a hectic world at arm's length.

From King's Quay the coast trends northwest to Old Castle Point, one of the twin northern tips of the Island's diamond shape (the other is Egypt Point on the west side of the Medina estuary). This is a beautiful shore to sail along and the gentle curve of Osborne Bay is usually sheltered except from northerly and easterly winds. The foreshore rises steeply and abruptly from a thin line of rough gravelly beach, clad in a covering of trees that look as if they stretch for miles over the hill that hides Osborne House and well inland. Barton Wood and Pier Wood show not a roof or a sign of habitation, and for this short stretch the island shrouds itself at its most mysterious and uninhabited. Osborne Bay is, for good scenic reasons, a popular anchorage. Cowes, just around the corner, is hidden by the woody bluff of Old Castle Point. Eastward, the richly wooded coast stretches away to the outskirts of Ryde, which the peace makes much farther away than just a few miles. The curve of the bay gives safe anchorage well out from the shore, which is advisable because the shoals, and some choice example of Isle of Wight reefs, run out here and there. At low tide they are dark, seaweedy shadows beneath the surface, with small fronds of weed breaking the surface at low water springs and giving some warning. For exploration closer in, a shallow draft boat, especially a centreboarder, is yet again at an advantage.

For yachts standing well offshore, beyond the Middle Banks and on the north side of the deep channel, the tops of two Italianate towers might just be glimpsed over the dark mass of Barton Wood, one of them topped with a flagstaff. This is virtually all that can be seen from the Solent waters of the building which was once the centre of the Empire. It was planned by a young royal couple as their dream home in the 1840s, and when Queen Victoria and the Prince Consort moved in in 1845 they set the Island on a new course. Revolving, you might say, around Osborne.

They needed, in the Queen's words, 'A place of one's own, quiet and retired'. In those days, even more than in the intrusive present, royalty could hardly move abroad without being mobbed and jostled by crowds. The Queen had known and loved the Island from childhood, so with the Solent as a broad moat and a house set in broad grounds, the dream of somewhere 'quiet and retired' yet within easy travelling distance of London became practical. A short walk down through the trees and the couple came to their own bathing beach. A small gatehouse stands between the shore and the woods, still known as Queen Victoria's Teahouse. There was bathing there, too. An apparatus was constructed at Portsmouth Dockyard which could be raised and lowered by cranks, to afford a dignified dip into the briny for a royal bather. And the view offshore was rather fine. On the then undeveloped mainland side four miles away, the summits of the South Downs rise in the distance above the well-wooded Hampshire coastal plain, and away to the left one could see the whole length of Southampton Water with the New Forest on its western bank.

For those who care to join the summer pilgrimage of visitors, Osborne House seems thoroughly and confidently early Victorian, Italian architecture adapted to the cool and uncertain climate of the Atlantic seaboard. Today the fashion of deriding everything Victorian is itself old fashioned, so that it is quite acceptable to praise the place, which is rather fine.

The Italianate style was all the rage when the Prince Consort called in his favourite architect and builder Thomas Cubitt to extend the small Georgian house which previously occupied the hilltop site. The Prince, who loved having a go at things practical, is said to have designed it himself, incorporating such novelties as fireproofed materials. The Italian style is not out of place: the eastern Solent even today can stand comparison with the Bay of Naples, and the square-topped towers and balustrades blend well with the landscape, as the Royal Victoria Hospital, the other great memorial to Victorian taste which once fronted Southampton Water at Netley, did in its own parkland setting. Osborne was no passing fancy so far as Queen Victoria was concerned. After the death of Albert at Windsor in 1861 she reigned almost continuously from her Island home until on a January day in 1901, surrounded by accumulated relics and photographs of her beloved family, she died, bringing the longest reign in British history to a close.

The new King, Edward VII, not surprisingly, had not the same affection for the place and he promptly gave it to the nation. The household wing was converted into an officers' convalescent home, and for some years naval cadets served two years' prep there before they went to the Royal Naval College at Dartmouth. Two young naval persons who did their two years there were the future King Edward VIII and King George VI. Today most of the house is open to the public, and one of the strongest impressions from a visit is that the commonly maligned Victorian taste was not so bad after all. There are features that it's hard to come to terms with, like a room decorated with animal horns, but even today Osborne would still make a residence worthy of members of the royal family.

Just over the hill to the southwest, where the land slopes gently down to the tidal valley of the River Medina, stands another monument to the Prince Consort's interest in architecture. However, when he rebuilt Whippingham Church, which stands on a Saxon site, as the parish church of Osborne, he went for the German style instead of the Italian. Albert Jenkins Humbert, a Southampton architect, assisted and the result features a singular mixture of the remains of the Gothic revival introduced by Nash when he redesigned the church in 1804 and the German pinnacles favoured by the Prince Consort. 'Both ordinary and pretentious' is one critic's assessment of it. Today we tend less to patronise things Victorian, having had time to assimilate the features of modern architecture, and welcome the church's jolly individuality as un-ordinary.

Just to the west of a gate half hidden in the trees, which led to Osborne's private beach, a sudden break gives a dramatic first view of the third interesting building along this short stretch of coast (a flourishing monastery, a royal residence and a lived-in castle is not a bad show in the space of three miles). Norris Castle really looks the part with its squat, pseudo-Norman presence. But it fails to look severe; perhaps its pleasant parkland setting makes it seem a comfortable and friendly sort of place. Norris makes a change because it is nothing to do with Henry VIII, or the pair of castles he built at East and West Cowes. It was designed by James Wyatt and built for Lord Henry Seymour between 1795 and 1805, when the creation of romantic replicas and Fonthill-type follies was a lucrative line of work for architects.

But there is an air of the real thing about Norris, more than is usually found in surviving Georgian reproductions. Inside there are flagged floors and stone staircases which could have made a perfect setting for Errol Flynn and Basil Rathbone to battle it out in *Robin Hood*. But Norris is a comfortable home, not a museum. Several royal guests have stayed; George IV was there and so was his sister-in-law the Duchess of Kent, and

Norris Castle

Osborne Bay

her young daughter Princess Victoria, in the 1830s. The young princess's lifelong love of the Island was probably nourished by the happy summers she spent here, with the woods and seashore offering adventurous explorations, and occasional sailing expeditions.

Victoria was so fond of the place that she made a bid to buy the castle, unsuccessfully, so that Osborne House was chosen instead as the setting for her Island home. The Seymour family sold the castle to the Duke of Bedford in the 1880s when his wife was appointed Mistress of the Robes to the Queen, and Norris still made royal visitors at home until the turn of the century. One was Kaiser Wilhelm II of Germany, then a regular Cowes Week visitor. To make his visits happy a special bathtub was installed, equipped at one end with a screened shower, some years before its time, by which the royal bather could spray himself either sitting or standing. It was remembered in the household as a deadly contraption which squirted boiling water in all directions. The Kaiser, ever the macho, had a nude portrait of a Miss Banks, a Cowes lady friend, hung so that she looked down on him as he bathed.

From 1903 there have been five owners of Norris Castle. Mr Birkbeck, who owned Harrods, had it until 1951. Today it is the home of Mrs Jonne Lacon whose mother, Mrs Catherine Briscoe-George, bought it from Birkbeck. Mrs Lacon, the wife of a naval officer, has embellished the castle during her residence until it is, as she said a little while back, 'full of stuff my family has collected over 400 years'. Mrs Lacon has re-established the surrounding estate and opens the place to visitors on an informal basis three days a week. 'We never set out to be really commercial,' she explained, 'and the day opening the castle ceases to be fun and becomes a bind, that will be that.' These open days, which began in the '70s, seem to be in abeyance at present. But whether the house opens again for visitors or not, the young people of Cowes and district have a friend in Mrs Lacon, who allows them to use the Norris grounds for gymkhanas, Scout and Guide camps and other jollies. At the foot of her domain, where the lawns and trees slope down to the water of Osborne Bay, Norris Rocks extend from the shore, an underwater trap for the unwary who steer too close in when the tide is low, and who can be stuck there until it turns again. There is a lovely story that the lady of the house had been known to take pity on stranded mariners whom she recognised, and have refreshments sent down to ease the wait. When I put this to Mrs Lacon she disclaimed the credit, but added that it could have been a bit of Norris hospitality practised in earlier times.

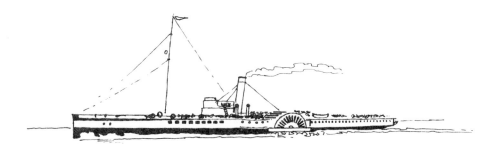

Approaching Cowes

2 Cowes and Newport

THE name Cowes, source of many a feeble pun in its time and which upper crust yachties pronounce 'Ca-hawes', is said to derive from the two forts, called 'cows', which Henry VIII, the enthusiastic fortifier of Solent harbours, had built on each side of the mouth of the Medina. The western one survives as the foundation of the Royal Yacht Squadron's headquarters and starting platform. North from the Squadron's battery of brass cannon, so trustingly left on their seafront emplacement, runs the most famous yacht race starting line in the world. At some time or other all the most competitive yachtsmen from around the world have jockeyed here in a dignified (sometimes not) pre-start mêlée for races which might take them just around a Solent course or way out into the Atlantic. From the flagstoned promenade which curves to the west below the Squadron's battlements is the finest place anywhere to study the mysterious but skilled ritual, the strategy of nicely judging time and distance, the aim of which is to give a yacht a good start which in such keen competition could decide the outcome. The corner is packed for the start of important races. But there is a magic in the place on quiet days. Just to walk round the corner from the shelter of West Cowes parade and feel the first invigorating touch of a westerly bellowing up the Solent is one of its more robust delights. What makes the spot such a good place for spectators is that from here they can enjoy the nautical scene in a way pretty well unique along the South Coast: with the sun shining from behind. The effect is magic on a bright clear day, when the characteristic emerald of the Solent seas is tinged with blue and grey and topped with sparkling white crests, with the long low treeline of the mainland shore making the background. The tides run strong here and there is deep water close in, so the brave show put up by small boats on a lively day can be enjoyed at close range from the comfort of the dry but draughty land. Cowes has never been short of critics of its shortcomings as a place to watch round-the-buoys racing after the starts. A somewhat illogical grouse, this: after all, racing, as the lavishly staged America's Cup battles off Fremantle demonstrated, is still essentially a participation sport. Yachtsmen themselves would agree with the old grumble of one sports writer, perhaps a bit out of his depth, that to the mere spectator it was a pastime like watching the grass grow. But in yacht racing the experts tend to be out there getting on with it, and not airing their knowledge from a seat in the stands, and the arrival of on-board television seems only to have confirmed that. What Cowes offers is more exciting: a seascape second to none, adorned by the magnificent sight during the Week of those vast fleets running back under the pretty spinnakers from a windward mark which, if it happens to be out of sight down the western end of the Solent, only adds to the fun of seeing how the field has changed when they reappear. Those who come only for one week of the year and find fault with the place for its lack of four-star accommodation, and quiet night life, are really saying nothing new, and what's more, they miss the point. The real business of Cowes has always been out there on that tricky tidal water and though new hotels and restaurants have come onto the shore scene in recent years, that still applies. As for the town itself, which for 50 weeks of the year has to earn its living without the aid of the world's yachting elite, it is Cowes, warts and all, good enough for kings and emperors in its day and in our more democratic times, and still the Solent harbour where small boat sailors can feel they have really come home.

Yachts don't have it to themselves. This is the Island's one deep-water port, and at East Cowes there is the Trinity House depot where buoys and

East Cowes Marina

Cowes Week

Keelboat moorings in Cowes

seamarks for the area are serviced. The old name for Cowes, before the
forts, seems to have been Shamblord, surviving perhaps in the name of
Shambler's Copse on the high ground above West Cowes. The Island's
real cargo port before the growth of vehicle ferries took the trade from
motor barges and gave it to lorries, was four miles upstream right in the
centre of the capital at Newport. Rows of warehouses, many now refur-
bished for leisure activities, line the old quays where barges from
Southampton and Portsmouth used to take the muddy bottom when the
Medina River dropped to a trickle at low tide. Across these quays, where
yachts now lie, virtually all the Island's bulk cargo trade passed until less
than 30 years ago.

A sail up the Medina from Cowes is well worthwhile. Above Cowes,
gently rolling countryside slopes down to the water on either side. Near
high water the river glitters broad and blue on a sunny day, but it shrinks
sadly when the tide is away, so for a quick turn-round visit to Newport the
tide table is important. Allowing for the fact that this is a short water link
between two towns, the tidal river makes a pleasant voyage.

Newport and Cowes had their respective roles: Newport as the cargo
terminal, Cowes for the building of craft and the servicing and provisioning of visiting ones. Ships of all sorts still anchor beyond the roadstead,
which in the days of sail might be packed with vessels sheltering from bad
weather outside or awaiting a fair slant of wind for an outward-bound
voyage down-Channel. The Cowes watermen were kept busy, particularly

The Trinity House Wharf in East Cowes

during the Napoleonic Wars when convoys mustered here, attending to their needs.

Cowes was also the Solent's main Customs port. In 1777 William Arnold took up his appointment as Collector of Customs in the town, and through his zeal and intelligent observation of his adversaries, the smugglers, is still honoured in the Service as one of its finest officers. He lived in a house in Birmingham Road, West Cowes where a red tablet on the wall records the birth in 1795 of the famous father's even more famous son: Thomas, who was to become Dr Thomas Arnold, Headmaster of Rugby and the mentor of *Tom Brown's Schooldays*. What was so remarkable about

The Folly Inn on the Medina

William Arnold, at a time when smugglers were popular heroes, as well as very tough customers when crossed, was his integrity. He was incorruptible at a time when sweetening a palm was the accepted way of unofficial business. He worked long hours and, when the Service turned down his requests for more revenue cutters to intercept smugglers' vessels, he paid for one out of his own pocket. She was the *Swan*, which foundered in a gale in Hurst Narrows just a month after Arnold commissioned her. But it seems that the Admiralty, if not the Board of Customs, was impressed with Arnold's efforts, and sent in a cutter to patrol the waters between the West Solent and Christchurch. By 1786 Arnold had put the Island smugglers so much on the defensive, with his cutter patrols afloat and mounted officers ashore, that he actually drove many out of business. Arnold later became the Deputy Postmaster for the Isle of Wight and collector of light dues for Trinity House. The hard life he set himself took its toll and he died suddenly in 1801 at the age of 55, almost certainly of overwork. He was buried in Whippingham churchyard, just back from the Medina upstream of East Cowes; his memorial tablet extolled him as 'A man who, by his amiable, as well as by his faithful, discharge of his duty in his public station and private character, justly entitled him to the warmest esteem and affection of all . . .' Perhaps the smugglers themselves even had a sneaking regard for such a worthy adversary.

A famous landmark for yachtsmen for many years has been the Folly Inn, a pub standing close to the water in a rustic setting about halfway from Cowes to Newport. Today its riverside is packed with boats, but a dinghy can usually nose in for its occupants to test the place's hospitality or to take a walk half a mile across the fields to visit Whippingham church.

For the more energetic who don't mind missing a tide, the distance to Osborne House itself is no great trek from the Folly.

Some factory buildings just downstream of the Folly are a monument to Isle of Wight pioneering in aircraft technology. Here the Osborne Plywood Works between the wars turned out vast quantities of the material for use in the pioneer flying boats built at the Saunders-Roe factory. On the opposite side, about a mile below Newport, are the remains of a cement works which once contributed to the Medina's brisk barge traffic. In the days of the Island's steam railways the line from West Cowes to Newport hugged the west shore of the river for most of its length, so that cheery waves between engine footplate men and small-boat crews were part of the fun of a voyage upstream to Newport.

One used to arrive in the heart of Newport by river, and the centre of the town and its shops were just a short walk from the quays; not that yachts were encouraged, the barge traffic being so busy, but there was room downstream to anchor, in a boat that could take the ground, with a short pull up to Newport by dinghy. A wide road bridge now overshadows the quays, part of a through-road system which as in so many places has meant ripping a large hole in the centre of the town. East and West Cowes are luckier in this respect because they are not really on the road to anywhere else. Newport, on the other hand, as the geographical centre of the Island is a busy crossroads, hence the need for this urban road system to cope with traffic, although nobody with time to spare and a boat of suitable size would join in this rush (just like anywhere else's) when there's a chance to enjoy a quiet voyage of exploration up such a delightful river.

When it is possible to arrive by sea at a town one has not visited before, it is an awful waste of an opportunity to do it any other way. And for the collection of charming small towns that line the Solent, almost unforgivable. Cowes is a perfect example. Arrive by ferry if you must, in your own boat if you can. Adlard Coles, I think it was, advised small-boat sailors never to scorn riding on a ferry as a good way of reconnoitring unexplored waters. Leaning on the rail of one of the Red Funnel ferries that ply to and from Southampton, the good sense of this advice is immediately clear. However, it applies to the old-fashioned ship ferries where you can walk around topsides and stare; the hydrofoil service is a swift boon to people getting somewhere quickly on business, but the view from its windows is not a patch on that to be enjoyed from the upper deck of one of Red Funnel's *Castles*. The hydrofoil takes 20 minutes, pontoon to pontoon; the ferry takes an hour. On a fine day in any but the coldest months of the year it's an hour well spent. One of the first things that strikes the practised eye is how the two bold headlands that flank the River Medina mouth, and on which stand West and East Cowes, protect the Solent's most sheltered harbour against the prevailing south and westerly winds and, to a lesser degree, from the southeast. On both sides of the estuary the high, woody bluffs can shut out the breeze as if somebody has closed a door. A yacht approaching Cowes in a good westerly breeze can be laid over to her lee gunwale and romping through a lively turn-of-the-tide lop in the Roadstead, where the tidal streams run strong and the Prince Consort buoy has a bow wave as if it is being towed by a submarine. Then, as the land looms up on the starboard hand, the boisterousness ceases suddenly and, in what has become little more than a gentle breeze, a boat progresses sedately to her mooring, if she's a local, or to the Ancasta Marina if she's a visitor. Conversely, when it blows from north or northeast Cowes is dismally vulnerable. Sizable seas roll into the harbour mouth, and surge against the landing stairs at the Royal Yacht Squadron, testing the skill of any launchman arriving there and set on making a dignified touchdown. Farther upstream the pontoons of the Island Sailing Club fret and groan against their restraining timber pile uprights; across the river, the lines of moored boats on the moorings just within the Shrape breakwater rise and pitch in worried fashion.

On a good high tide seas surge playfully over the undulating paving outside the Royal Yacht Squadron, cutting off the walk to Prince's Green to anybody without gumboots. Waterside shops and houses are exposed to the draught, and windcheaters are the dress of the day for members who enjoy a drink in the open on one of the club balconies.

Two handsome houses attract attention upstream of the Island Sailing Club's pontoons, each with its own small jetty and each the epitome of a sailing man's waterside home. One, close beside the Harbour Lights pub, used to be owned by Uffa Fox, Cowes born and the town's best known sailing son. A good yarn-spinner in the best nautical style, Uffa was a leading pioneer of the concept of fast-planing sailing dinghies. But he used to say that the job which brought him most satisfaction was designing his airborne lifeboats for war service. These double-enders, beautifully built of laminated wood, were intended to be dropped from aircraft to ditched airmen. But the workmanship that went into them earned several a new lease of life after the war when, in those timber-starved days, they were eagerly bought up as war surplus and gave many owners years of good service when converted to small cruisers or day-sailers. Uffa's 'disposable' boats proved very durable.

Almost next door, and similar in style, stands Prospect House, perfectly named, the home for many years of Sir Max Aitken, who was not only one of the town's leading yachting personalities but liked the place enough to live there for long spells. When Sir Max died part of the house was turned into a museum of curiosities connected with his family – like the gold and ivory dirk, formerly Hitler's, taken from the Berlin bunker and given to Stalin who in turn passed it on to Sir Max's father, Lord Beaverbrook.

You can tell the Cowes natives. When they step from their front doors of a morning they inspect the sky and assess the weather. It's a habit cultivated for a practical reason, because they are sailors themselves with a plentiful programme of afternoon and evening races to be enjoyed in the less hectic season each side of Cowes Week. Ask the postman or the milkman early in the morning for the weather forecast and he'll give it to you fluently. Apart from the summer entrepreneurs who shut up shop when the crowds go, the all-year-rounders make the place welcoming; they understand small boats and their needs, and they know about good seamanship and will smile indulgently at a bit of swank without being impressed by it. The sailor among them is among friends.

It's a tradition that goes back far before a group of gentlemen met in a London hostelry in 1815 and decided on a summer muster at Cowes once a year to enjoy some yachting and waterside socialising. What may have largely influenced those founder members of the Royal Yacht Squadron was that the port was already well used by naval and Customs cutters, which used to take part in off-duty racing in the roadstead. Cowes' sheltered deep-water harbour must have weighed in its favour. Given the advantages of the sheltered Solent and its comparative ease of road access from London, they would have been hard put to choose anywhere else.

Newtown Creek entrance looking east

3 Cowes to Yarmouth

SETTING forth from Cowes on a westward passage always seems to have a sense of zestful adventure about it. Maybe it has something to do with leaving the more domesticated eastern half of the Solent, once a boat leaves the seaside Cowes suburb of Gurnard astern. The western Solent isn't any wider than the eastern half, but it looks it. A good beat to windward from Cowes towards Yarmouth or beyond, on a bright day when the spray glints with rainbow colours over the lee bow, has the spacious sense of being at sea but with the presence of a choice of easy harbours within reach. A small boat coasting along the Island shore provides her crew with the satisfying sight of several miles of virtually deserted beach in front of low cliffs, these backed by rolling farm and woodland rising gently to the Downs on the horizon. To the north, on the mainland side, hardly a rooftop shows above the low-lying woods, giving the illusion that the New Forest starts close to the shore and goes on for miles. Together, both shores along this seven miles produce some of the most beautiful estuarial scenery around the English coast, for its marrying of distant hills and coastal plains.

This way has been the start of countless voyages over the years from Cowes, Southampton or Portsmouth, bound west away round the world or merely catching the tide for a peaceful night's anchorage at Newtown. Herbert Alker Tripp, who wrote in the 1920s about an easy-going meander around the Solent in his barge yacht *Growler*, captured the zest of that passage, closehauled against a westerly breeze and with the weather-going tide setting up a lively sea which in the West Solent seems that more lively wherever the wind comes from.

35

' . . . For one moment the clouds rifted somewhere, and let through a single shaft of sunlight. The glitter of light was like a charm; the whole seascape was brought to life by it. After that, gradually, the clouds became detached masses of white on a sky of blue. The wind had not moderated and the weight of the seas was unchanged, but the waves lost their vicious look at once. Under blue skies they were no longer formidable, and the spray which still swept us at moments had lost its sting.' This might apply to most tidal estuaries on an outward-bound passage, but seems to capture the mood of the West Solent to perfection.

Herbert Alker Tripp was as good with a pen and brush as he was with words, and embellished his classic of Solent cruising, entitled *The Solent and the Southern Waters*, with his own drawings and watercolours. Classic because aboard his 32 foot barge yacht *Growler II*, which served him well for 30 years or more, he explored the Solent of the 1920s at an easy pace. Those were days before engines ruled and when people – in books anyway – never seemed to hurry; if you were becalmed you anchored, lit pipes and spun yarns. If the tide set against you, you turned to the nearest creek, confident in those happy uncrowded days that there would be plenty of room to lie to an anchor. Sir Herbert (he was knighted in 1945) joined New Scotland Yard in 1902 at the age of nineteen, and rose to become Assistant Commissioner of the Metropolitan Police in 1932. Policemen can be poets, and lovers of peace and quiet like any other man, and Alker Tripp's book smiles with enjoyment. Only once does his professional background make a fleeting appearance, when he sailed *Growler* into Poole Harbour and took exception to the notice boards he saw ashore, stating that 'Trespassers will be prosecuted' and so forth.

'As trespass, apart from wilful damage, is no offence', he wrote, 'prosecution is impossible – the remedy being a civil one.' He castigated the more high-flown language of signs saying 'The Police have strict orders' etc. as an even more flagrant mis-statement: ' . . . but both are still freely indulged in by landowners'.

In this litter-lout age, it is less easy to feel aggrieved at landowners' attempts to keep places clean and decent. Happily, local authorities on both sides of the Solent are realising the tremendous following for the pastime of country walking. Landowners also seem to be realising that a clearly marked footpath will help prevent the straying they fear so much. On both sides of the Solent, the efforts of the respective county councils to improve scenic footpaths and keep them clearly marked have earned them praise.

Sir Herbert, who remarked of Newtown that it was 'a pleasant place to anchor' might now be happy to know that, since the National Trust took the place under their care about 25 years ago, it has a good chance of staying that way. Sadly, the pressures on the charming anchorage have become such on high summer weekends that boats have actually been

Newtown Creek

crowded out. Anchoring outside can be attractive enough in settled weather, but it makes for a long run ashore if the crew insist on the customary visit to the New Inn at Shalfleet which lies (if Newtown's collection of creeks can be likened to a spread hand with the narrow entrance as its wrist) at the southern tip of the forefinger. At less hectic times the magic of the place is as the skipper of *Growler* would have known it. Rarely can the pleasures of 'port after stormie sea' be so enjoyed as steering into Newtown after a tussle with the West Solent on a breezy day. The clamour and crash of waves dies away. When a boat has sought and secured a suitable anchorage there comes that end of a yachtsman's day which is only just removed from heaven, when pleasantly tired after a strenuous day he can relax in the cockpit of his boat, watching night fall across land and hearing little more than the plaintive call of wading birds, the distant lowing of a cow in a field some way away, or the occasional distant thrum of a ship's diesels as she passes outside, beyond the shingle bank which makes a natural sea wall against the open Solent.

Newtown itself, today just a hamlet tucked away down a lane, is one of those places which enhance their attractiveness by having come down in the world. This was once Francheville, the Free Town, a flourishing port in its day and at one time no less than the capital of the Island. When the Danes arrived in 1001 for some rape and pillage, it was probably called Wealtham. It recovered from the attentions of the Norsemen and was prosperous enough to be granted charters by Henry III and Edward II, his being for a three-day fair, vigil and feast each year. Then came disaster. In the cross-Channel gang warfare of the 14th century several Solent towns, even Southampton so far inland, were raided by the French. When they landed at Newtown in 1377 they destroyed it completely.

Newtown looking seaward

There was a brave attempt made to revive the place. It was laid out in the formal style of the New Town its name perpetuates, and today leafy lanes bear such townie names as High Street, Gold Street, Draper's Alley and Kay (Quay) Street. Along these at one time merchants thronged. Newtown finally gave up the ghost as a town in 1832, when the Reform Bill robbed it of its Rotten Borough status. The previous year a census had counted a population of 68. One of its most famous MPs was John Churchill, later Duke of Marlborough: I wonder if he ever visited it.

One building in particular survives to echo Newtown's former dignity, the Georgian Town Hall, the subject of an odd restoration project in the 1930s. A group called the Ferguson Gang, anonymous philanthropists who went about doing good deeds in masks, restored the building and handed it over to the care of the National Trust. Some years ago a set of fine carved chairs was removed and given a new life in the Isle of Wight County Council chamber at Newport.

Newtown Creek is an important nature reserve, which is not immediately apparent to the visitor by water as the wardening is efficient but discreet. The 300 acres of woodland and saltmarsh in the centre of the cluster of creeks is one of the best areas for naturalists in the whole Solent area. It was founded as long ago as 1919 by the Isle of Wight Natural History and Archaeological Society, long before such projects had the support they enjoy today.

Red squirrels, hardly to be seen any more on the mainland, can be glimpsed in the woods along the north shore and, in the tradition of islands having at least one exclusive species, the Wight has the butterfly Glanville's fritillary. Wild flower enthusiasts can find the wood calamint which is rare across the water. Oyster beds are laid in Clamerkin Lake and lower downstream in the Newtown River. Several moorings are laid in the deeper channels, so short-stay visitors would do well to buoy their anchor. This lovely place just begs to be explored by dinghy. On the upper reaches of the creeks dense trees on either side effectively rule out sailing, and as the noise and pong of outboard motors would shatter the peace of the surroundings, Newtown is an ideal place to rummage out the rowlocks and rediscover the lost art of rowing. For this, of course, you need a proper boat, not an inflatable, which have put numerous people unfairly against rowing for life.

As recently as 100 years ago Newtown Creek was rated as the best harbour on the Island, and vessels of up to 500 tons were said to ply there; somewhat hard to believe, looking at the narrow streams which trickle over the mud at low water today.

The vital approach mark from seaward is a small unlit red buoy. Never be tempted to make a short-cut inshore of this when approaching from the east: the shoals run a long way out from the entrance. From the west the approach is slightly easier, but from Hamstead Ledge buoy, where the tide seethes when running strongly over a submerged shelf, it is a good idea to hold course for the small red buoy, and not turn south to make the entrance until the leading marks inside can be laid. The pilot book wisely suggests an entry as early on the flood as possible, the best time to observe where the deep channels lie, to be hidden later. Cruising dinghies and centreboarders can take some liberties, but don't forget to look for notices warning of oyster beds. Immediately within the narrow entrance the main channel splits into several tributaries within the space of a few hundred yards. First, bearing away to port, is Clamerkin Lake, which runs far inland to the southeast, among peaceful looking downland which in fact bristles with Ministry of Defence danger areas, but a lovely cruise nevertheless. Farther south the channel divides again, Causeway Lake bearing to port, the route for visitors to Newtown Village and Shalfleet Lake to starboard. Shalfleet Creek runs straight southward to Shalfleet village – Newtown Creek's nearest approach to urban civilisation, and a very pretty village of brown-grey stone – and has another short spur called Corf Lake leading from it to port, just north of where the westernmost of Newtown's water rambles, the tree-screened Western Haven, wends off to starboard. Plenty to explore, then, for those of a peace-seeking disposition. A hint for newcomers to the delights of Newtown: don't try to cover all of it on one visit, save some unexplored reaches for another time.

Beside the New Inn at Shalfleet, well patronised by sailing folk during the season, there is a village shop for replenishing stores. For those who prefer provisioning ship in more of a holiday spirit, the farm on the west side at Lower Hamstead is said to provide water and fresh provisions. For anybody a bit worn by the strains of life, two or three days of lazy living aboard a small boat, with good air to stimulate the appetite and a walk to the New Inn for a spot of beneficial exercise, could do wonders. Be warned, though – it's a hard place to leave.

West from Newtown the island shore gradually loses the wide open appearance it had to the east, when the Downs soared up as a background to woods and farms. Bouldnor Cliff, rumpled like a giant unmade bed, subsides until at Bouldnor itself the main road from Newport to Yarmouth appears on the seafront, with houses and gardens; there is the grey stone of the castle at the water's edge and the neat square tower of the church announcing Yarmouth, the saltiest of Solent shore towns and the favourite of most cruising yachtsmen. Crews of large yachts probably venture no farther than the tiny but amazingly commodious harbour. But for the owner of a small centreboarder with a mast that can be lowered without fuss, the Western Yar itself is there to be explored, upstream of Yar Bridge, winding through saltmarsh and downland to within less than a mile of Freshwater Bay at the back of the Wight. The Western Yar nearly cuts off the western tip of the island as the Eastern Yar does the eastern, but the former is unembanked and tidal for all of its length. Because of this, the idea of Freshwater and Totland breaking away as a small island of their own seems less fanciful than a similar sundering of Bembridge from Brading.

Yarmouth, as its snug, well-settled look when seen from the sea suggests, is one of the oldest of Island towns. In the 14th century when cross-Channel raids by the French were a constant peril, Yarmouth, the westernmost and therefore most vulnerable of Island towns, had its share. It was attacked and burned in 1377, the same year that Newtown was destroyed, and ravaged again by the French in 1543 when only about half a dozen houses were left standing. Henry VIII, not a man to stand such daring insolence, included Yarmouth in his programme of defensive castles built along the Solent shores. Yarmouth's, beside the ferry terminal, looks quite domestic with its tiled roof and a pub on one side. The place was still garrisoned as late as 1885. Conveniently close, typical of the compactness of Yarmouth, is the George Hotel, a favourite call for visiting

yachtsmen, and once the residence of the Governor of the Island. This was Sir Robert Holmes, one of the Wight's most colourful characters. In the town's attractive church there is an ornate monument to the man, who had governed the Island in the reign of Charles II. He served under Prince Rupert in the Civil Wars and had a hand in winning New Amsterdam from the Dutch and renaming it New York, in honour of the Duke of York, the King's brother. The monument in the church commemorates another of his exploits. It is said that, on the hazy borderline between privateering and piracy of those days, a ship owned by Holmes captured a French vessel. In the hold was a sculpture of King Louis XIV on which, for some reason, the sculptor had not completed the head. Perhaps he was waiting to work on an authentic likeness. Holmes kept the statue, had his own face carved in place of Louis' and with a masterly piece of one-upmanship provided himself with a memorial fit for a king.

For sailing visitors (and townsfolk – Yarmouth's boat-owning population must be the highest for its size in the Island, except maybe for Bembridge and Seaview) the compact harbour is popular because there is no long estuary journey between it and the sea. Behind the old breakwater, which looks like a venerable garden wall topped by a wooden fence, is the open Solent, just a few yards away. But the tides run strongly past the tiny entrance: a boat trying to make it in a light breeze on a flood tide can be in danger of being carried onto the pier, which runs out from shore a few yards to the east. Happily for everybody, the ferry that links the town with Lymington on the opposite shore, berths just inside the entrance so that, provided it is given a free passage in and out, it is in no danger of being hampered by moored yachts, as can happen on the mainland side.

Yarmouth lifeboat, with its own mooring for a swift getaway, shares the harbour with the yachts. An RNLI boat was first stationed here in 1924, away from Totland Bay where rough weather could make launching arduous. Today the Yarmouth boat, which has to face the rough wind-against-tide conditions of the Needles Channel on most of its launches, is the successor to the rowing lifeboats, which used to be launched by men and horses – and rowed heroically clear of the steep breakers – round the corner at Brightstone, facing directly into the booming south-westerlies on the open Channel shore. Between them, the men of the Bembridge and Yarmouth boat crews leave rescue work within the Solent, which usually involves yachts and small craft, to their colleagues who man the inshore rescue craft stationed at Lymington, Southsea and other places. Their beat is on the open Channel, and both face singularly ugly seas where the jutting wedge of the Island interferes with the to-ing and fro-ing of the Channel tides. Many is the yachtsman jolted from sleep in his bunk by the thunderclap of the maroons fired from the lifeboat station bursting immediately overhead. These rouse the whole town, so that the Yarmouth lifeboat never puts to sea without an audience.

Today the ferry is virtually Yarmouth's last link with commercial shipping. In the 19th century colliers sailed direct from the northeast coast to bring coal from Newcastle and elsewhere to the town. The last to visit regularly was the *Rapid*, of Hartlepool, which discharged its last cargo in 1907. Another profitable trade was the loading of sand from Alum Bay for Cheshire, where it was used in making glass. This petered out in the last century when the glass makers found that a more suitable grade of material could be obtained from France. Sealink's modern ferry, painted in breezy holiday colours, has a tenuous link at most with the small hissing paddler that was taken by Alfred, Lord Tennyson for his comings and goings to the mainland when he lived at Farringford, just outside Freshwater. It was on that vessel, sailing from the little Lymington River into the open Solent bound for Yarmouth, that he conceived his simple but elegiac poem *Crossing the Bar*. Had he done the crossing a few years earlier, it is unlikely that the Poet Laureate would have felt in the mood for composing verse: until the 1830s the crossing was done in open rowing-sailing boats. In one fatal accident in 1837 a 23 foot Yarmouth boat capsized in a squall, and ten of the twelve passengers were drowned.

The ferryman's name was Webster. The agony of the event, and the resulting inquiry into the accident, must have been softened for him when he was praised for having held up a child (sadly, she died) and for holding on to the mailbag which his boat carried. Yarmouth owes its snugness as a harbour to the slender breakwater. It dates from 1843 and in the private enterprise spirit of the day several local people contributed to the cost, principally Mr G. H. Ward, one of the leading Isle of Wight worthies, of Cowes. He contributed not only cash but 5,000 tons of stone for the job. The Admiralty, possibly with an eye to Yarmouth's possibilities as a harbour of refuge, contributed some hundreds of wooden stakes, and an expert to advise on driving them. Everybody was pleased with the result except those of the town's longshoremen who had kept up the old but declining traditions of smuggling. For years past, before the new breakwater was built, they had been able to slip in discreetly by small boat onto the Norton sandspit, which still exists at the far western end of the harbour. The new breakwater meant they had to come in through the narrow entrance, right under the eyes of the Coastguard and Excise men. Not that everything the Corporation did pleased everybody: on one occasion a bit of high-handed action nearly caused a riot, as recalled by Captain A. G. Cole in his history of the town, published in 1950.

It seems that the Corporation had ambitions to make the harbour area more respectable. They had already fallen out with seamen and fishermen for what were claimed to be exorbitant dues, both for landing fish and for passage above the swing bridge into the upper Yar. In 1877 the town decided to limit access to the pier by fitting gates which were locked in the evening and on Sunday, and also barred people from getting down to the shore. The response was dramatic: armed with axes and sledgehammers, a band of seamen smashed down the gates, watched by a large crowd. It was morally right but legally wrong, and the Corporation took legal action against the leaders to reclaim the cost of the damage, only to find that the men's fishing boats, gear and possessions had been mysteriously sold to friends and relatives.

Through the early months of 1987 Yarmouth was putting up with chalk dust and the clatter of machinery as work on the new swing bridge over the Western Yar took shape close alongside and upstream of the old. Its wooden carriageway had stood up nobly to years of hammering by ever-increasing road traffic. Upstream of the bridges the Yar winds through a lovely mile or so of meadow and woodland up to the northern slopes of the Downs, well worth a voyage of exploration by dinghy on a tide.

The River Yar

4   Yarmouth to the Needles

ACROSS the Yar Bridge, the hard-worked gateway to the West Wight and the resorts around Freshwater for the summer multitude of visitors arriving by ferry from Lymington, lies Norton, the detached suburb of Yarmouth. From there the coastal cliffs start to rise, gentle and tree-clad at first, eventually to the multicoloured grandeur of Alum Bay and its sands and on to the great white jawbone and jagged teeth of the Needles. On Sconce Point stands Fort Victoria, an undistinguished 19th century structure built on the site of a much earlier fort called Carey's Sconce. Half a mile to the west is Cliff End, marked by the more substantial Fort Albert standing directly opposite Hurst Castle on the mainland side, but it is at Sconce that the sheltered water of the Solent really ends and the Hurst Channel begins with its fast tides that rush through the narrow bottleneck (they are the fastest in the Solent except for the spring ebb seething out of Portsmouth, Langstone or Chichester). The speed and power of the stream can be seen from the beach just west of Norton. Sconce Point buoy, a little way offshore where the deep channel skirts the land by a matter of yards, builds up a white bow wave and a bubbling wake, doing the equivalent of five knots through the water on a spring ebb.

Along the coast from here to the Needles there are some pleasant bathing beaches, but the stretch of water offshore of these is no place for novice sailors to venture in small boats, or indeed for swimmers to strike out too far. From Norton to the Needles, and around the corner past Scratchells Bay to the little chalky cove of Freshwater Bay, there is fine coastal walking country, with the giddy view of the Needles far below from the high spur of chalk above Alum Bay. Freshwater is of surprising

Looking across to Hurst from Fort Victoria

size, but it withdraws discreetly back from this magnificent bit of coast and the Downs are bare and free. Resorts like Colwell Bay and Totland Bay on the northern side give the impression of being detached, small places, spared the invasion of usual seaside tat. Up aloft, overlooking the tumbling dunes of Headon Warren and the West High Down, the wind sings through the short downland grass, the sea thrift makes the cliff edges bright with pink flowers in May, and if you are up there early enough on an autumn morning, you might find mushrooms for breakfast.

Fishing in Hurst Narrows

The Needles lighthouse, standing so close under the land, looks less than the daring structure it is, built on a mere toehold of chalky rock on the western tip of the outermost molar of the Needles. All around, when a gale torments the water as it fights the tide, can be observed one of the most unpleasant patches of sea around the coast. At Portland the seas are far worse, of course, but there the wild race is way offshore, half a mile from the Bill, and you need binoculars to see its mad leapings. Here the tidal stir comes in close, right to the foot of the light tower which then looks a tiny and lonely thing in bad weather. Its jaunty red and white bands, dwarfed by the vast wall of white which swoops down to it from 300 feet to sea level, ought to be more of a symbol of homecoming than it is. The white cliffs of Dover are pretty tame in comparison and anyway their significance is only to cross-Channel passengers from the Continent. There are few approaches from seaward grander than the Needles passage, but the approach to the Solent through those tide-swept narrows was ever tricky. The number of large vessels coming in this way has steadily diminished in favour of the eastern Nab entrance, and except in good conditions yacht skippers bound out for Cherbourg tend to favour the east-about route past Bembridge.

The Needles light is low, for a practical reason. Ancient lighthouses, which gave little more than a ruddy glow of burning coals in an iron basket, were placed high on clifftops. But the hope of showing the glimmer over a longer range was too often vitiated by the low sea mists that hid them from sea level. That is why Beachy Head light stands in the water below the cliff, instead of on it.

The granite tower of the Needles, 80 feet high, marks the eastern end of a breach in the chalk which stood from Purbeck right across Poole Bay. At the western end today, Old Harry Rocks near Swanage mark the western end of the breach. The long west coast of the Island, from Freshwater Bay down to St Catherine's Point, has been the scene of innumerable ship-wrecks right up to modern times. The most famous casualty at the Needles, however, has left large parts of herself for mariners to beware of. Just off the tip of the rocks, right below the lighthouse, lie the remains of the Greek freighter *Varvassi* which went aground there in January 1947 with a cargo of wine and oranges. In clear weather she ran onto the submerged ledge that extends from the base of the lighthouse and was broken into four sections, which still lie there. The most inshore piece, her boiler, just breaks the surface at low water about 100 yards west of the light. There's a natural hazard nearby called Goose Rock which is often mistaken for a part of the wreck. Between them they pose a strong dissuasion for craft to pass too close to the light on their way down the Back of the Wight.

Slap in the middle of this tide-sluiced channel lies another hazard, the Shingles Bank which shows above the surface at low water although

Alum Bay

sightings indicate that its area is rather less than it was. One of its unpleasant characteristics is that it sounds as cheerless as it looks. In even quiet weather the swell disturbs the shingle, the rattle and clatter of which is a distinctive sound. There is no playing around with the Shingles. Some hero may have landed on the bank from a small boat at some time during an exceptional spell of quiet weather, but not here the ritual games of hit-and-miss cricket like those on the Brambles off Cowes. The bank is rarely free of a swell, hardly felt in a boat on deep water nearby but breaking white upon it. But it is well buoyed and well feared, so that few people seem to pay the price of getting too close.

The currents between the Shingles and the Island shore have a characteristic which coasting sailors have long been aware of. On the ebb, the stream sets from Hurst Narrows straight towards the Shingles. On the flood it trends in towards the Island shore with its bays and offlying rocks. Lack of sea room and those formidable tides are the reason why big vessels favour the eastern end for approaching and leaving the Solent. In 1954, when Southampton was still a busy passenger port, somebody did a count and found that of the 3,093 large vessels entering the Solent, only 640 passed Hurst. Today the traffic is yachts and fishing boats, probably numbered in tens of thousands a year, which shows that the Narrows is not a fearsome boat-eater.

The high land hereabouts has always been a good grandstand for watching the ships that pass, and a fleet of yachts beating out, short-tacking in a westerly breeze, can make a stirring sight. The largest such passed that way on a cold and drizzly May morning in 1986 when more than 1,500 yachts taking part in the Island Sailing Club's 50th Round the Island Race were strung out in a close-packed procession that took hours to pass. Motorboat aces, with plenty of power at their fingertips, have been known to short-cut between the Needles rocks themselves when there is plenty of tide under their keels. Audacious, but not likely to leave locals impressed. They know how bad the place can be.

The Narrows, uncongenial to sailors, promised an unexpected benefit to the Solent in 1967, when the tanker *Torrey Canyon* ran aground off the Scillies and threatened to pollute the coastline as far east as the Isle of Wight and beyond. An emergency committee, chaired by the late Earl Mountbatten who was then Governor of the Island, announced a plan for a floating boom between Hurst Spit and Fort Albert, less than a mile away. There was a touch of Mountbatten flair and decisiveness about the idea which may have masked practical snags. Fortunately, it was not needed. But there have been other tanker accidents since and the Mountbatten Barrier might have to be tried yet.

5 Hurst to Beaulieu River

COASTING from the west, making a passage from say Poole, the built-up shoreline of Bournemouth and Boscombe goes on for miles until the great sandstone bluff of Hengistbury Head juts out, a welcome touch of the untamed after all the buildings. Actually, Hengistbury had a narrow escape from becoming the setting for the most grandiose edifice in the whole area. Between the wars Gordon Selfridge, of the Oxford Street store, had the idea of doing a Citizen Kane and building his own version of Xanadu on the bluff, a millionaire fairytale castle with turrets and what-not. He got as far as commissioning Philip Tilden (1887–1956), one of the most fashionable architects of the time, to draw up plans. Tilden also had another commission: to design a mighty tower for Selfridge's store. This too came to nothing. Now that we are learning to live with holiday home estates, caravan parks and conurbations of chalets, it's worth reflecting that if we are to have our coastlines bordered with buildings, the occasional bit of style might be no bad thing to break the monotony. For those who feel really anarchic about the growth of seaside clutter, a word of thanks is due to the Army, whose firing range along the Dorset coast to the west has kept the holiday home blight at bay.

Running out from Hengistbury and calling for a bend in a course shaped from Poole Harbour to Hurst Narrows, is Christchurch Ledge. Small craft cut inside the buoy which marks the end of it, 2½ miles offshore, and although the tides in Christchurch and Poole Bays are gentle by comparison with those of the Solent, a jolly lump can arise when the stream wells up over the sunken ledge. I have been through it in a sailing dinghy a few times without discomfort. The thing to watch out for here when sailing close in, as with most patches of offlying rocks, are the buoys marking lobster pots. One of those around a propeller can cause acute embarrassment. After Hengistbury the great whaleback of the cliffs behind the Needles begins to look awesome. From a small boat it is like being an insect stared at by a dinosaur.

On the mainland side, the villas of Highcliffe and Milford on Sea take up most of the space. Then there's another welcome break as the gravelly shore starts its great curve to the south, ending dramatically in the white castle and twin lighthouses on Hurst Spit. Small craft favour entering the Solent by way of the North Channel, standing in for North Head buoy before steering parallel with the last mile of the Spit. There's one hazard to watch out for before turning the boat's head east into the sheltered water of the Solent. It is well named the Trap – a small but vicious patch of overfalls just southwest of Hurst Castle. Daring centreboard folk steer close to the spit and get away with passing inshore of the Trap. Strangers might find that a dummy run or two in kindly weather is helpful before trying this. Reading pilot books and their warning of tide-rips, overfalls and so on can be as daunting for the cautious sailor as reading medical books can be for the man who worries about his health. The thing to remember is that these places are perilous in breezy weather, as anywhere is on tidal waters. If you are lucky with your weather, and show a bit of respect, Hurst Narrows need be no more frightening than Cowes Roads. The first time I passed west of Hurst, in a 12 foot dinghy, was on a gentle summer morning, with the sun burning up the mist revealing the Purbeck Hills floating in the sky to the west. The breeze was light easterly, but I rounded up in Hurst Roads and tied in a reef. After all, this was big stuff, going outside the Solent for the first time in one's young life. So it was a sedate exit. Far too sedate because away to the southwest the impercept-ible swell was breaking on the Shingles even in the near calm. A bit of steerage way to keep clear of that was obviously a good idea. So, assuming a pose of sangfroid and listening all the while to the merry rattle and gravelly roar on the Shingles, I rounded up and shook out that reef. Once you're out, of course, in a boat of that size thoughts tend to persist of what conditions will be like for getting back, when the first of the flood tide begins to speed up and confronts a bit more breeze from the east. Both happened, but the little boat swooped gamely through the Narrows gateway leaving her young skipper time to observe that phenomenon of the tideway off Hurst, the Pinnacles. These are not rocks but small waves rising up in pyramid shapes, something like goose-pimples. A hundred and fifty feet below her keel, the old ebb was becoming the new flood. Engaging reverse gear was somehow the cause of those spiky waves.

For the crew in no particular hurry and who can afford to idle away a fair tide, anchoring in Hurst Roads is a pleasant way to stop and reflect on one's first passage of the Narrows, and hereabouts the scenery well

Keyhaven

deserves more than the passing glance that a busy crew can spare from a boat under way. With the wind anywhere west, there is good shelter here with little risk of mealtime crockery being upset. A really small boat, such as a cruising dinghy, can follow the winding channel up to the little harbour at Keyhaven, where there is a pleasant pub, helpful boatyards and a short walk to shops. The place gets as busy as any other waterway deep enough to float a boat these days, but at Keyhaven the boats, like the background, are smaller and things seem more easy-going than in one of the bigger estuaries to the east. For those who prefer to stay put at anchor in the roadstead, there is the sight of the Island Downs and the Needles and, on the mainland side, broad acres of saltmarsh backed by stocky wind-bent trees. Lying quietly here, a skipper with a whole holiday ahead can look eastward, past the canebrake of masts in the Lymington River and red-roofed Yarmouth clustered about its church on the far side, and anticipate pleasant days of exploration in sheltered waters.

On days not so good, there can be great satisfaction in lying fairly snug under the lee of Hurst Spit, as a westerly blow creams up the Shingles like a meringue mix and large boats in the Narrows dip and rise, snorting spray from their bows. One can land on the spit itself and watch the steep Channel breakers pounding on its outward side. In shape and ingredients it is like a Chesil Beach in miniature; and, as at Chesil, there are occasional anxieties of it being breached. The effect on the Solent, especially on the wildlife rich saltmarshes along the north shore, would be catastrophic. Heaps of brick rubble and building stone which can be seen dumped at various spots along the western side show where reinforcement has been applied to prevent the shingle bank wearing dangerously thin. The danger of a breach seems to be greatest at the northern end where the spit meets the land. A disastrous winter gale could imperil Keyhaven, so the dumpings of man-made material are specially important along here. Some blame the dredging of gravel and aggregates from the West Solent for sapping the spit. To prove the connection would need long and detailed surveys by hydrographers, and to mount this sort of operation would require what the Solent Protection Society has long called for – an overall body to study causes and effects on the Solent as a whole, instead of individual local authorities having to look after their own territories piecemeal. Hurst Spit itself has a breakwater: the Shingles Bank, which breaks the worst of the seas in southwesterly weather. There have been suggestions that the Shingles is not as big as it was. Finding the reasons and implications of that, if true, would pose an even more complex problem for the experts.

Hurst Spit widens out at its southern end and curves eastward like a crook on the end of a long handle. The eastern edge of this crook, about a mile from north to south, forms that ideal short-stay anchorage in westerly weather, the Camber. It is still as John Scott Hughes described it 30 or so years ago, one of the most fascinating spots in the Solent. Although he qualified it, even that long ago, as 'a little too frequented'. Keyhaven in high summer is not only a little frequented but well stocked with moorings, so that the best way to get there is by dinghy, either under sail or oar. This used to be a small working harbour in those days when trading craft would nose into the smallest inlets to load or discharge cargoes, and today, although the coasters have gone, Keyhaven has a sizable fleet of fishing boats. In the summer months visitors can board a ferry for the voyage down the sedge-lined Keyhaven Lake to Hurst Castle. More energetic souls can get to the spit just west of Keyhaven and walk the length of it. But, like any long trudge on shifting gravel, this can be hard work.

As a destination, Hurst Castle itself which looks quite fine from the sea, is barely worth the effort. It was originally built as part of Henry VIII's grand design for coastal protection along the Solent shores and a pretty God-forsaken place it must have been then. The stone for Henry's original part was obtained from Beaulieu Abbey after the Dissolution, a bit of architectural vandalism beside which those of the 20th century pale. Idleness following the receding of the danger of raids by the French led to the Castle falling into disrepair. Its moment of fame came in the Civil War, when it was occupied by Parliamentary forces. It was to this miserable place that Charles I, after a year of reasonably polite imprisonment at Carisbrooke Castle, was brought in November 1648. The King, it was recorded, was 'slenderly accommodated', and that must have been some understatement. He was kept here for nineteen days before being taken to the comparative paradise of Windsor in time for Christmas. When he arrived at Hurst he had just over two months to live.

The place fell into obscurity again until Victorian times, when the two colonnaded wings were added in response to another French invasion scare. By 1933 the military had decided they had no use for it and bestowed it on the Ministry of Works (now the Department of the Environment) and it is now preserved as an ancient monument.

For sailors, however, Hurst is much more than that. Standing close to the castle buildings is the tall, white-towered High Light, so called to distinguish it from the stumpy red housing of the Low Light, built onto the castle itself. Between them the two lights in line give a transit bearing for the approach to the Narrows. Keyhaven Lake, the little channel which curves round the tip of the Hurst crook on its way in to Keyhaven, is joined just before it reaches that place by Hawker's Lake, coming in from the east. It was named after Colonel Peter Hawker, a Regency character who must have been one of the greatest exterminators of birdlife of all time. Colonel Hawker discovered Keyhaven marshes as a wildlife haven and later had a cottage built there. He seems to have spent most of his time thereafter blasting away at anything that moved, braving the worst of winter weather in pursuit of game. According to Barry Shurlock, 'It has been calculated that during the period 1802–53, he took 29 species of bird, including 1,327 Brent geese, 2,211 wigeon and 1,329 dunlin. It is perhaps surprising that there are still as many wild birds to be seen at Keyhaven as there are . . .'

It's hard to imagine, on a visit to charming Keyhaven today, that it narrowly escaped being involved in one of the more grandiose schemes for a link with the Isle of Wight. In 1901 somebody suggested that about a mile inland from here a rail tunnel should be dug to the Island. Yet another invasion scare was in the air about this time, from Germany, which did one good thing – it helped to inspire *The Riddle of the Sands*. Anyway, the tunnel scheme came to nothing. In fact, quite a lot of schemes for turning various parts of the Solent into large modern docks have, thankfully, come to nothing over the past 100 years or so, or in the case of Buckler's Hard on the Beaulieu River, much earlier.

One of the delights of arriving at Keyhaven by dinghy is that the boat can be hauled up in sheltered safety beside the waterside path just below Keyhaven Sailing Club. For those who feel they can qualify, the Keyhaven hospitality is famous. Just as famous is Keyhaven's pub, The Gun, which actually has a small cannon, believed to have been recovered from the sea, on top of its front porch.

Depending largely on the protection of Hurst Spit is an enormous area of saltmarsh foreshore, running eastward from Keyhaven about seven miles to the Beaulieu River entrance and about a mile in depth at its western end, gradually tapering to Needs Oar Point. These virtually undisturbed miles form a great nature reserve where seabirds and other creatures can go about their business with few intrusions from humans. The main breach in this coastal belt is where the Lymington River winds up to this pleasant town. Approaching it from the Solent you can tell where Lymington is from miles away, not from the buildings, which are surprisingly well screened by trees from the sea, but by the extraordinary mass of yacht masts which gleam in the sun and which on a clear day can be seen distinctly on the other side of the Solent at Yarmouth. Lymington is a yachtsman's town, like Yarmouth, but it has paid for its popularity by surrendering more river space to lay moorings, so that today its boat population on the river and in the new marina near its mouth is staggering. Through that mass, several times a day, is performed a minor masterpiece of seamanship as the Sealink vehicle ferry comes and goes. The effect of her passing causes a spectacular phenomenon, especially about half-tide. The water displaced by the ferry's hull falls back astern of her at such a speed that shallow draft boats are left for several seconds high and dry on the mud. Then there is a sort of rebound, as the displaced water surges back across the mud to restore its own level, and picks up the boats it had so recently abandoned and sets them tossing on a miniature turbulence. The ferry skippers are wonderfully tolerant of the press of craft which shares the river with them, but sound moorings are a must to withstand the jostle as they pass slowly by. The stretch of the river that passes through saltmarsh on its way seaward is much longer than that bordered by Lymington itself. For a good two miles that seagrass persists on either side of the channel, gradually becoming thinner and more threadbare until deep water is reached at last, heralded by the marks with jolly names which are a feature of navigation at Lymington: the Cocked Hat, the Tar Barrel Post, the Bag of Halfpence and, the outlier of them all, Jack in the Basket. With Jack abaft the beam, you are at last at sea.

Lymington is the most elegant of the Solent-side towns, with that rare attribute, good building that does not degenerate into scruffiness near the water. I'll stick loyally to my own favourite, little Yarmouth across the water, because Lymington, even by the crowded state of Solent rivers, gets pretty packed. But once safely on a visitor's mooring or in a marina berth, the town shops, chandleries, pubs, picture galleries and boatyards provide for every need. There are coaching-inn hotels, shop fascias on which shopkeepers still devote care and expense in having their names and businesses painted in elegant gold letters, and the town has the good manners to end properly instead of in a straggle of the overgrown sheds of the typical industrial estate.

Long before the needs of tourists were taken seriously, this was a town of consequence. In 1345 it mustered more ships to ferry Edward III's Army to France than Portsmouth, and about that time was collecting more Customs receipts than Southampton. One commodity, however, was pre-eminent in Lymington's commercial story: salt. Walk down the west side of the river today, towards the new marina, and the traces of grid-pattern low walls surrounding large flat ponds can be clearly seen. Into these seawater was run and allowed to evaporate naturally as much as possible. Then the strong, thick brine was pumped into pans and boiled over coal fires, to produce the final crystalline salt. In 1800 Lymington was producing as much salt as was being shipped through Liverpool from the Cheshire salt mines (which still provides that used on roads in winter to this day), but that was its peak. A heavy salt tax and a tax on coal destroyed the profits from the trade and by 1865 the last salt pan was closed. As Lymington historian Edward King described it, 'the industry, which lined the shore with a busy population and covered the channel with fleets of merchantmen, had now totally ceased, and left the marshy coast silent except for the whistle of the plover or the whirr of the wild duck . . .'. Today we see it as a social tragedy when great industries close down after barely a century of activity. Set against this the fact that the production of salt at Lymington had been going on for no less than 700 years and by 1800 was producing a tenth of the nation's requirement. It went to Newfoundland to salt cod and into the salt pork of the sailing navy, and into such products as Epsom and Glauber Salts for medicinal use.

Soon after the death of the salt industry came an idea of developing the Lymington River downstream of the town as a major deep-water port. It got as far as an Act of Parliament, which made provision for the Lymington Harbour & Dock Company to build a dock and a tidal basin on the present site of the peaceful Pennington Marshes. If the project had got off the ground, it would have meant the development of the river well inland of the town as well. Fortunately it failed. The reason possibly being that Southampton had got in first, with the building of its enormous Docks beginning in earnest in the 1840s, so interest in the Lymington scheme withered.

The Salterns

Upstream of Lymington today the navigable river comes to an abrupt halt with a great dyke which carries the road from Lymington Town across to the ferry terminal on the east side. This puzzling barricade, which denies the town a large tract of navigable water upstream, is due to a quirky 18th century character called Captain William Cross, a seaman, who took it into his head to build the dyke, lay a road on top and charge people for passage. What is more, despite huffing and puffing by the town council, he was allowed to get away with it, and brandished a musket at anybody who dared approach with the intention of tearing the structure down. Upstream the river quickly began to silt, and today produces a vast area of rich, tall reeds. Various court cases connected with this unorthodox bit of private enterprise (let nobody rail against our modern planning legislation!) went on for years. People obediently paid their pennies right up until 1967, when the Corporation took over the rights and tolls were abolished. Many river folk in Lymington heartily wished the dyke had been abolished with it, and if the pressure of mooring space in the lower river continues to grow, it might be worth a look at the idea of reopening the upper river to the tide. But a careful assessment of the effect this would have on wildlife upstream would have to be made before justifying the scheme.

Rising above the trees above the east bank is a rather handsome stone column on Walhampton Hill, in honour of Admiral Sir H. Burrard Neale, an early 19th century worthy and benefactor of the town; he stumped up for its first gas lamps in 1832. On the Walhampton side the shore trends away eastward. Some nice houses are set back comfortably among the small oaks and tamarisk trees that grow almost sideways from the constant pressure of the wind off the sea. The shore, unapproachable by sea because of the marsh, and privately owned on the landward side, is one of the most peaceful stretches on the Solent.

A couple of miles east of Lymington there is the merest trace of waterside life at the foot of a delightful lane which runs from the village of East End to the sea, past verges cropped by the grazing New Forest ponies and attractive red-tiled cottages. Alas, the place is now known to too many motorists who make a clutter at the seaward end in the season. A tiny creek, Tanners Lake, runs in from seaward and provides a haven for a small collection of fishing and sailing dinghies. I hope it doesn't get spoiled, but the attraction of the place can be understood. It's the only bit of public access to the water between Lepe and Walhampton, and short of imposing a 'residents only' restriction on vehicles, there seems no way to preserve its charm.

About half a mile inland from the shore, and running roughly parallel with it is a tranquil lane which serves the farms of the area. The lane, which also is the route of the Solent Way long-distance footpath, is bordered by hedgerows which are considerately kept trimmed to a

Tanners Lake

pedestrian's chest height. It's probably a happy accident rather than the intention, but this low hedge line allows a continuous splendid view of the Solent away to the south and to the Island beyond. Along this lane, before the traveller comes to the magnificent ruin of the great barn of St Leonard's, there's a reminder of the French connection established by the monks of Beaulieu in their day, in a farm called Bergerie east of Sowley Pond. Today it's a bird sanctuary, and a more peaceful, private one is hard to imagine. Yet in the days of the sailing navy, when ships were built at

Sowley

Buckler's Hard, this was a place of heavy industry. There was an iron-works here where the iron fittings for the ships were made.

This little road is an example of why it is such a good idea to stow a couple of folding bikes aboard a cruising boat, which can be used for a bit of serendipity ashore. After the bustle of Lymington the quiet, broken only occasionally by a passing car or farm tractor, is a rare experience. The only man-made sounds to compete with the caw of rooks and the cough of pheasants or the bleat of sheep might be a tractor at work in a field or, when the wind is off the sea, the soft, faraway drum of a ship's diesel.

The two sides of the Solent along here are similar, but not too alike. Here, on the Beaulieu Estate, the fields, hedgerows and farm buildings are of apple-pie neatness, interspersed with small spinneys of stocky oak trees, mossy in the fresh sea air. Two or three miles away on the Island side the low-lying foreshore is richly forested with these same stocky oaks, with small farms far away from the nearest main road. Both sides of the Solent are ideal country for a bit of exercise on those bikes carried folded in the yacht's fo'c'sle.

Still travelling eastward past Sowley, and with the lush woodland that borders the Beaulieu River already in sight ahead, one comes suddenly upon one of the glories of English monastic building. Not sacred, just a barn. But what a barn. The old walls of the original now contain a smaller, newer one. This used to be the grange of Beaulieu Abbey and the two gable-ended walls show that the barn was 216 feet long, about 60 feet high and about as wide. The amount of New Forest oak that went into roofing that immense span must have been enormous, and the craftsman-ship of getting it up there quite wonderful. Happily, the great barn is what it was intended to be, part of a workaday farmyard scene. There has been no attempt to mummify it as an ancient monument surrounded by mown grass. Its grass-topped walls look all the more magnificent because of that.

6 Beaulieu River

COMING eastward by sea, the first sight of bright needle masts against the dark screen of trees inland reveals the Beaulieu River, although there is some little way to go yet before its evasive entrance reveals itself. Sand and shingle spits that trend eastward from the mouths of estuaries are a familiar feature of the Solent. Hurst Spit has that eastward twist at its end; there is a more substantial example at Calshot where the shingle wraps a protective arm around Ower Lake. Tiny Titchfield Haven is formed by this persistent eastward shift also. But Beaulieu is slightly different because it seems that the river itself has had to change its course to accommodate it. The course of the river, from its birth in the peaty streams that run from the boggy New Forest heathland, is fairly straightforward until its last mile. From its sources to Beaulieu itself the river is elusive; an insignificant stream overgrown with trees for most of the way, and so small as to be hardly worth a glance where a road bridge crosses it. At Beaulieu there's a sudden and beautiful transformation as the stunted stream sweeps into the broad expanse of the Mill Pond. Reeds fringe its banks and the buildings of Palace House and the mill reflect grey and red on its broad surface.

This unexpected and beautiful view of the little town never fails to delight first-time visitors arriving by road from Southampton or Lyndhurst. For two miles or so, as the road winds among trees and marsh the river has no more than hinted at its presence. Then trees cease all at once and, like a curtain drawn back, they reveal the cluster of old red brick and russet tiles, and that lovely mere with its grassy banks trimmed to garden lawn neatness by the Forest ponies. But this is only the first half of

Beaulieu

the transformation of Beaulieu River. From the Mill Pond, follow the road as it curves to the left into Beaulieu, turn left at the Montague Arms and within a few yards one of the finest Solent river views opens out on the right: the first reach of the now tidal, fully grown river, with a richness of mature trees bordering its banks. Even at low tide this sudden transition from forest stream to tidal waterway is stirring; at high water, when the outstretched branches of the crowding trees seem to skim the surface, this effect is magic. The road here is narrow with a couple of blind bends so there is no encouragement for that most dismal of pastimes, parking and staring through the windscreen.

Motorists can enjoy it better by parking at the western end of the village street and walking back. Bring a bag of bread scraps, because the ducks are very appreciative. Better not to let the ponies see what is going on, however. They can turn a bit nasty if they are refused food, and to give in to their demands means leading them into bad habits, such as saunter-ing across busy roads when there is a prospect of titbits. Palace House, built on the remains of the 13th century Cistercian abbey, looks grand from here.

Dividing the Mill Pond from the tide is a gem of a mill house, and across the water on the west side, up a little cul-de-sac, is, or used to be, a small boatyard and chandlery. I spent a blissful summer there one year as general painter, varnisher and dogsbody, splicing ropes' ends for people accustomed to having such things done by others. On one occasion we had to strip and re-varnish a launch which was to be used by the Duke of Edinburgh on a visit to Calshot. An important arrival in the post about that time was the Duke's personal standard which we had to bend on a staff and fix on the foredeck. Over this happy place was a majestic elm tree. We never got on, because it used to rain seeds and debris on any varnish one was unwise enough to attempt in the open. Palace Quay Boat Yard did a good trade in fibreglass versions of the old Solent scows, dainty 10-footers with a balanced lugsail and spoon bow. A surprising number of them are still around, 25 years on.

But back to the river. From Beaulieu it winds, as all the best rivers do, holding back the view around the next bend, only to reveal another bend hiding another view. Buckler's Hard is on the last but one of these bends. Once past Gilbury on the left bank, it suddenly straightens its course towards the Exbury shore a mile downstream. Off Gins it turns southeast as if heading for the open Solent. But no, it turns east-northeast for its final mile, running parallel with the Solent but divided from it by the bird sanctuary of Gull Island until, off Lepe, the channel does a perfunctory right turn into the Solent. For most of its course from Beaulieu, the river is magnificently wooded, the trees open here and there to give glimpses of fine houses at the far end of magnificent gardens, blazing in spring with the colour of rhododendrons and azalias. Near Gins the woods give way gradually to saltings. To the south and west of Gins there is a large tract of fields and many small pools and ditches, providing wetland habitat for water birds.

The Beaulieu River

Gull Island – an island no more

The river, and wide tracts of land on the west as far as Sowley and east as far as Cadland, form a site of major importance and much of it has now been declared a national nature reserve, through agreements between the Nature Conservancy Council and the Beaulieu and Cadland Estates. Here is enlightened private landownership at its best, with good husbandry coupled with a generous respect for the rights of wild things to live lives of their own. Don't expect to visit the area and be invited to stroll through sensitive areas as if they are city parks: that's not the way of nature reserves. Those of us who are not dedicated botanists or ornithologists need just be glad that these acres are there, adding a touch of remoteness and mystery to this lovely shoreline. The jewel in the Solent's crown, the river has been called. That is probably still true, but I would say that Newtown must run it very close, carat for carat.

But even Beaulieu River has that problem which besets every creek and harbour of the Solent: how to cope with the boats which require moorings without becoming just another packed marine garage? Just after the war there were a few moorings upstream of Buckler's Hard, but not many. Today, shallow draft boats and bilge-keelers, which can take the ground at low water, occupy the shallow reaches up as far as Oxleys, almost within sight of that grand first view extolled earlier. Downstream there are moorings flanking the broadening fairway to the bend beyond Gins, where the Royal Southampton Yacht Club has its sailing station. Thankfully, not everything is sacrificed to yachts and their needs.

At its last bend, where the river runs for its last mile inshore of Gull Island, there was for many years a swatchway separating the island from Needs Oar Point. It was supposed to have been dug by a local character in the 18th century as a convenient way of leaving and entering the river without the detour. Bull was his name and he started more than he knew. His cut, even as recently as the 1950s, was fairly narrow, so that Bull Run (a more macho version of its original name, Bull Lake) was used as a short-cut only by people with local knowledge. But in recent years the channel widened enormously and seemed set to become even wider than the original river mouth at Lepe. As it grew, Gull Island began to diminish and there was growing fear of it eroding away, with serious effects on the Exbury foreshore. Bull Run ceased to be an adventurous short-cut and became a main channel. They even buoyed it, and it was even wide enough for a fair-sized yacht to beat in against a northerly breeze. Concern grew, until it was decided that the Run would need to be closed to prevent more erosion. The Beaulieu Estate had to seek Parliamentary approval, because Bull Run constituted a navigable waterway. There was some opposition, and even the Royal Yachting Association took a close look before deciding that closing the gap was in the best interests of the river. The necessary approval was granted and work on closing the Run began in 1986, making Gull Island, which had lost about a fifth of its area since the Second World War, an island no more.

The Beaulieu River's great attraction for visitors by sea or road is Buckler's Hard, a fragment of 18th century industrial town planning which was to have served a port which never materialised. Later it became the most important private shipbuilding centre in the Solent area. Today it is unpretentiously beautiful, the beauty carefully preserved by the Beaulieu Estate which, while providing visitors with what they need like car parks and loos, has kept these amenities carefully apart from the two rows of Georgian terraced cottages set each side of a broad grassy avenue sloping down to a bend in the river. Across the water to the east there is woodland that looks like a great forest going on for miles, with only the towers and chimneys of the Fawley Refinery to spoil that illusion. In other directions there are spinneys, farms and narrow lanes. How the place manages to maintain its character without being swamped by its own popularity is a little miracle. In the splendid Maritime Museum, which preserves memories of the hamlet's industrial past in the end building of the southern terrace, there is a magnificent detailed model, showing how it would have looked in its late 18th century heyday, when Henry Adams and his sons were turning out naval and merchant ships almost non-stop until the end of the Napoleonic Wars. Among them were the 64-gun *Agamemnon*, which Nelson declared was his favourite, and the frigates *Euryalus* and *Swiftsure* which served at Trafalgar. Today yachts cluster at the riverside end of the broad sloping street where these vessels slid down the ways. The Adamses built the hulls, which were then taken in tow by rowing barges to Portsmouth Dockyard for rigging and fitting out.

A permanent building yard like this, apart from those in the naval dockyards and along the London River, was something of a novelty in the days of Henry Adams & Sons. It was a time when a master builder might rent a piece of riverside foreshore with good timber within handy distance, lay a slipway and build a ship, probably just one, either for his own use or to order. If this produced another order, and if he got on well with the owner of the land, he might stay and build another. If not, or because a more attractive site was available elsewhere, he would pack up and move on. The first vessel to be built at Buckler's Hard was the 508 ton *Surprise*, launched by a Hythe entrepreneur called James Wyatt in 1745. But upstream at Bailey's Hard, on the west bank just below Beaulieu, Richard and James Herring had built the first ship on the river, the 682 ton *Salisbury*, in 1698. From the launch of the *Surprise*, until 1815 when the fortunes of the Adams family were in decline, 57 vessels were built for the Navy alone, more than by any other civilian yard in Hampshire or the Isle of Wight. Buckler's Hard would have seemed an obvious choice for the site of a settled yard. But as Alec Holland pointed out in his history of Buckler's Hard, the growing nationwide shortage of suitable shipbuilding timber as the 18th century passed meant that men like the Adamses (the

Buckler's Hard

father, Henry, was a timber merchant as well as a builder) might travel the country as far north as Shropshire looking for good stands. The royal dockyards, as the largest shipbuilding units, had the first choice of timber from the New Forest as they did the other royal forests. Later, as the shortage became more acute, timber imports from the Baltic and North America increased. So an independent builder, as well as needing faith in his ability to fulfil a naval contract on time and avoid penalties, needed a cool head to take risks when it came to arranging timber for delivery, which might take weeks of slow horse-drawn progress over the roads of the time. Pressure and stress are not known only to 20th century businessmen.

Buckler's Hard may look today like a carefully planned little community, expressly designed as a country shipyard. But John, the second Duke of Montagu, had greater things in mind for the site in 1722, when he obtained from George I a charter of proprietorship over the West Indies islands of St Vincent and St Lucia, claimed by Britain under the Treaty of Utrecht but the subject of a territorial dispute with the French.

Taking the risk of likely trouble with the French, Duke John embarked on a project to harvest and export sugar from his new domains and to ship it home to his own private port, sited beside his own river. Buckler's Hard was to assume the grander title of Montagu Town, with workers' cottages, wharves and quays. But first he had to settle a colony on the islands to get production going. He mustered a fleet and a band of colonists – a large number of ne'er-do-wells and jailbirds among them, probably – which sailed under the command of Captain Nathaniel Uring in September 1722, and by December 19 the Union Flag was flying over the newly named Montagu Point, now the site of the Vigie Airport near the town of Castries on St Lucia. But the days of the great venture were already numbered.

The flag went up on December 19 and the colonists enjoyed Christmas, killing and roasting a cow for their feast. But on January 7 the French, who had landed 18,000 soldiers on the island, made Uring an offer he could not refuse: leave or be thrown out. Uring took the sensible course and so ended the Duke of Montagu's hopes of a colonial empire. He had sunk £10,000 into the venture and all he had to show for it was the bare nucleus of the intended Montagu Town on the banks of the Beaulieu. He still had hopes for the place, but only a few plots were occupied piecemeal and the Hard lapsed until 1739 brought war with Spain and the usual wartime frantic demand for ships. It was a good time for the private builder, and James Wyatt, who was unknown to the Duke of Montagu, took the site. Everything was right at Buckler's Hard: the slope down to the water was just right for laying a slipway with a good depth of water; there was a quay for vessels to lie alongside, good storage space for timber and housing accommodation. Although he got shipbuilding going on the river, Wyatt decided to pull out from its risks and uncertainties and go back to his timber business. His successor was a Gosport man called Darley, then Moody Janverin of Hamble, and finally in 1748 a young ambitious shipwright from Deptford who had come south as a surveyor appointed by the Navy Board to survey some ships being built on contract. Henry Adams had arrived. His business was to be associated with Buckler's Hard during its busiest years until his death in 1805 at the age of 92. Despite the efforts of his sons, it did not long survive him.

Derelict industrial enterprises have a nostalgic charm sometimes, but on the Beaulieu River these have not left much mark on the landscape. There was a brickworks near the river until the 1930s and landing craft for D-Day were built along the banks. But the period that the river as a whole most seems to evoke is one that hardly changed its appearance at all. There's a sense of Edwardian elegance about the river and its craft – brash loud colours and contorted trendy shapes are not as widespread here as elsewhere – and visions of King Edward VII, or George V and Queen Mary arriving by steam launch from Cowes Week across the water for afternoon tea at Palace House come to mind very easily.

The river is wrapped round protectively by woodland against motor cars, yet it is only a walk away from the National Motor Museum, housing perhaps the finest collection of vintage vehicles in the country. One of the marvels of the Beaulieu Estate generally is that Lord Montagu, whose family name is associated nationwide with pioneer motoring, heads a team which has ensured that visitors' cars keep a discreet low profile on the estate's tourist attractions. At Buckler's Hard, for example, which had to have a car park to cope with the soaring number of visitors after the war, a quite large one has been sited round the corner and hidden from the broad central street.

Even in the 1930s the increasing yacht traffic off Buckler's Hard was making conditions cramped for the Beaulieu River Sailing Club, which had been formed in 1931 under the patronage of Pearl, Lady Montagu. In 1936 the club's landing pontoons were moved downstream to Gin's Farm; this became the club's sailing base, but its headquarters remained at Buckler's Hard until 1939. A stretch of grass running down to the river was dubbed, in deference to a certain establishment at West Cowes, the Squadron Lawn. BRSC sailing was a leisurely, friendly affair in those days, as indeed it was at so many small sailing clubs before competition became so important. Typical of the club's race programme was one which started from Lepe in the morning, stopped for lunch at Buckler's Hard, and carried the tide up to Beaulieu where there was a break for tea before the return to Buckler's Hard. Where, presumably, if somebody happened to raise the matter, they might discuss who had won.

John, the second Baron Montagu of Beaulieu and father of the present Lord Montagu, is remembered as the archetypal progressive Edwardian, an enthusiast for cars and motor boats. But his love of cars and engineering tend to obscure his skill as a sailing man, which he demonstrated at the ripe age of fifteen. He crept away from Palace House at dawn, having arranged to meet a friend at Buckler's Hard, and between them they satisfied John's ambition to sail around the Isle of Wight in a dinghy. When it was formed, the Beaulieu River Sailing Club sailed scows, still a popular type at several Solent sailing centres from Bembridge to Yarmouth. Later they commissioned a design of their own, the 15 foot hardchine Montagu Sharpie, the first of the class being built by Elkins (originally at Lymington, later at Christchurch) for £49 each. A larger 19 foot version was introduced in 1939, but the war came before it could become established. Stern restrictions were imposed by the Admiralty on small-boat sailing on the Solent during wartime, and some 50 Sharpies spent the war years laid up under the shrubs in the Palace House gardens, to be brought out of hibernation five years later.

Wise management has enabled this lovely river to withstand the attentions of its thousands of visitors each year. The Estate has to pay its way to survive, but what lifts the Beaulieu River and its hinterland into a class of its own are the quiet places, away from the tourist spots: tiny salt creeks or 'lakes', marshy grasslands, gravelly banks and clumps of acidy woodland; where wildlife, from the orb-web spinning spider to Brent geese, from yellow horned poppies and silver hairgrass to celery-leaved crowfoot and lady's bedstraw, could be the most worthwhile inheritance this generation can pass on to the next in an increasingly crowded world.

7 Southampton Water

SMALL-BOAT explorers miss a lot if they fail to include a voyage of exploration up the length of Southampton Water as part of their cruise. It's too busy, some say; others are put off because they have heard that it's all industry and docks. They are both wrong. Oddly, many regard the Hamble River as a place not to be missed. But a passage up the most crowded waterway on the Solent seems dreary stuff compared with what Southampton Water has to offer in the way of interesting things to look at. Southampton itself, six miles from the mouth at Calshot, always was a yachtsman's town and now, with the decline of commercial demands on its waterfront, is rapidly becoming even more of one.

And the rewards of a cruise do not end where the Rivers Itchen and Test divide. Beyond the long quay of the Western Docks on the Test side, it can be worthwhile carrying a tide beyond the new container terminal which crowds the fairway a bit, off Marchwood power station and the Magazine, past the tree-lined shores on the west bank for a look at the tiny and ancient harbour of Eling and its restored tidal mill. Beyond the container berths the Eling channel, and the harbour itself, drain almost to a trickle when the tides goes away, so that for a boat of any draft timing is important. On the top of the tide, a yacht might anchor just off the channel, visiting Eling by dinghy. But a watch should be kept for the working craft, barges and timber ships which use the channel to the wharves at Redbridge within Eling harbour. A centreboard boat is most comfortable in these waters. Over the past 20 years the Test estuary has been drastically reduced by dock extensions; before that it offered a broad tract of water ideal for dinghy sailing as far up as the low iron railway

Eling

bridge at Redbridge. A bit of local advice is worth seeking about picking up a short-stay mooring in Eling, or lying alongside a pontoon at high water. There are some shops nearby and, if time allows, a walk up the short, steep hill from the toll bridge is rewarding, to look around from the churchyard where a footpath runs down to the water at Goatee Shore. The church, St Mary's, is the oldest in the New Forest area, and it is believed that a chapel was established here in AD 850. It is said that the hymn writer Isaac Watts, a native of Southampton, was so taken with the view of Southampton across the Test (long before the days of dock reclamation) that he was inspired to write his lines 'There is a land of pure delight . . . .'. It must have been delightful then. But sadly, 'the sweet fields . . . dressed in living green' can now be seen to the west, where for just a mile or so between Eling and Marchwood there survives a glimpse of the tree-lined shores which, even well after the Second World War, made these waters such a beautiful haunt for small boats.

Eling Mill, which straddles the narrow causeway at the top of the tiny harbour, is a delightful building of red brick and tile, the sort of building, in the sort of setting, to make passing artists want to stop and unpack their painting gear. It is of immense age. A mill was recorded there in the Domesday Book when a Southampton man, Thomas Mydlington, leased the mill and toll bridge from its owners, Winchester College. The College

St Mary's at Eling

retained its ownership of the mill, which for several years after the war was the clubhouse of Eling Sailing Club, until 1975, when they gave it to New Forest District Council. The council carried out an extensive restoration and brought the mill back to working order. Visitors can actually buy flour there, milled on the premises. Before the war when the mill was in regular use, the scouring action of the water held back in the pond upstream until the turn of the tide helped to wash out the mud in the harbour. Spritsail barges used to find their way in here, as did topsail schooners. Today it is still a working harbour, with coasters discharging timber and road ballast at the tiny quay.

Southward, the great slab-sided mass of Marchwood power station dominates the view, overshadowing the low red-brick walls of the ammunition magazine built there in Victorian times in what was then an isolated spot. Marchwood village with its stumpy spire is inland a bit, but hard by the power station are the jetties and berths for which the village is known to British soldiers far and wide as the base of the Royal Corps of Transport's logistic landing ships. Husband's Shipyard next door overlooks Cracknore Hard, once linked by a small ferry to Southampton and not long ago graced by a Brickwoods pub, conspicuous and inviting, right by the water's edge. Dibden Bay, which used to curve westward from here towards Hythe, has been shrunk by reclamation and there is now a large housing estate where the New Forest used to straggle down to the shore. Hythe, once a tiny waterside village, is now vast, but the old waterfront remains much the same. The developments have been inland, the homes

Marchwood

of people who work in Southampton or in the petrochemical industries along the Waterside, as the west bank of Southampton Water is called. The real eye-catching newcomer on the foreshore scene is the marina, with a community of houses set around a series of small lagoons, each equipped with berths, where dwellers can enjoy the bliss of looking out of their front room windows at their boats.

Initial proposals for the siting of a marina here were first mooted in the late 1960s, and support for the idea grew steadily until the finalised scheme was unwrapped at the Southampton Boat Show in 1982. The marina is run by the same firm which established the Shamrock Quay Marina on the River Itchen on the east side of Southampton, where the Camper & Nicholson slipways and lay-up berths used to be. At Hythe, work began in earnest in the summer of 1984, the lock gates were in place by January the following year, the outer basin flooded in July 1985, and at the end of that month the work was far enough advanced for Chay Blyth to be invited to perform the opening ceremony. The architectural style of the marina's houses is pleasantly conventional, with no attempt at St Tropez trendiness which would have looked out of place here. Boat owners who berth here have spacious open water right outside the lock gates, and there is another advantage: just inland, the road specially built to handle the heavy traffic to the Waterside's industrial plants provides a quick link with the M27 motorway, which runs east–west around the north of Southampton.

Hythe Marina Village

The Southampton ferry terminal is at the seaward end of the pier, still doing good service as it has from Victorian times and enduring better than its spindly bird-like legs would suggest. It runs out a good half mile from the village, across the broad area of shingle and mud which largely dries at low water to a little way short of the deep channel. A walk along the pier's length can bring colour to the cheeks on a breezy day, and it is a popular grandstand for watching the passing of the big ships – liners among them still, occasionally – in and out of Southampton Docks across the way. But workaday folk from the Waterside, who depend on the ferry as a commuter link, and who have to use the pier in all weathers, are glad of the famous narrow-gauge electric train which connects the shore end with the ferries, making the difference between getting to work in comfort or arriving wet and wind-blown. The old ferry has moved with the times: today there is a smart vessel, all encased in tinted glass with comfortable seats. Great for the commuters, but something of a disappointment for holidaymakers who enjoyed pacing the open decks of the old *Hotspurs*. Inevitably, road competition has made itself felt on this ancient crossing (on Saxton's map

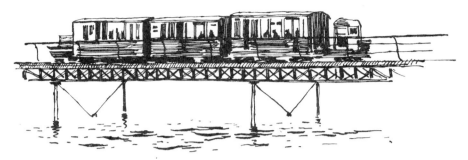

Hythe Railway

of 1575 it is marked as Hytheferye), and now only one vessel makes the journey instead of two, which used to start from Southampton Town Quay and Hythe Pier simultaneously and pass halfway. But its importance as a link for those Waterside people who have to travel to Southampton on business is such that it has received grants from Hampshire County Council. Hythe has one of the most flourishing sailing clubs on Southampton Water, one of those in the tradition of members themselves having done the hard work of building their clubhouse and its shoreside installations.

Hythe played an important part in marine technology between the wars, and in aviation even earlier. Where the big sheds stand along Shore Road to the south, flying boats were built in the First World War and in the 30s they were used as a maintenance base for the Imperial Airways flying boat fleet. This leisurely link with the Far East and Australia must have been a most civilised way to travel, with overnight stops at the best hotels along the way. Sadly, BOAC, as it then was, pulled out of flying boat operations in 1950. Shorter-distance services were kept going for a few years by Aquila Airways, mainly to Mediterranean resorts, but these ceased in 1958. In the Thirties Hythe was a centre for developments in another form of speedy transport. Hubert Scott-Paine set up the British Power Boat Company, which established the hard-chine, planing power-boat hull as a proven type for open-sea work. Working with Scott-Paine for a while was one Aircraftsman Shaw, trying to escape the limelight of having been Lawrence of Arabia, who carried out detailed practical trials of the launches over some four years which led to them being adopted by the RAF as the founders of the air-sea rescue fleet. With the seaworthy characteristics of his first craft proven, Scott-Paine went on to pioneer the development of motor torpedo boats. During his time with the British Power Boat Company, Shaw (or Lawrence) demonstrated that being a classical scholar was no handicap to a grasp of technical matters; he managed to combine the preparation of technical manuals on the Scott-Paine Class 200 launches with working on his translation of Homer.

From the water, much of the Esso Refinery complex and its associated industry is cleverly concealed by trees, north of where the silver tanks and jetties take over the shore opposite the entrance to the Hamble River. Just to the south, ages removed in spirit from all this technology, is the tiny harbour of Ashlett with the handsome red-brick mill which is now the Esso staff social club. Yachts are its traffic now, but this used to be a busy port of call for spritsail sailing barges and small coasters. It was the small port that served the pleasant village of Fawley which, amazingly, still remains pleasant – although cut off from the woods and fields that surrounded it until the early Fifties – despite the nearness of Energy City. At night it is bathed in the lurid glow of the Fawley flame, the oft-cursed glare of the waste gases which burn off from a tall tower over the refinery. To the south, the vast mass of Fawley power station dominates the skyline, representing the price we have to pay for energy at the touch of a switch, or useful materials made from petrochemicals, or the freedom of mobility brought by the petrol and diesel engine. Southampton Water has done its bit for the national good and deserves to be allowed to hold on to what remains of the pleasant green country that once lined the whole length of it.

Like a gatepost at the mouth of Southampton Water is the drum shape, characteristic of Henry VIII's sea defences, of Calshot Castle, standing on the tip of the spit formed by the eastward drift of shingle along the North Solent. Here again hightech had its day. In the Twenties the RAF High Speed Flight was based here for the Schneider Trophy races between the wars. For a long time in the postwar years, Calshot represented the end of a brave hope to re-establish flying boats as a sensible way of using big passenger-carrying aircraft, rather than take up tracts of land for the building of airports. Saunders-Roe at Cowes took up the challenge with their handsome Princess flying boats, but these were never given a chance to prove themselves. Somewhere, it was muttered, in some corridor of power, a faceless one had set himself against the flying boat concept and, if such things occurred to him, all the environmental advantages they might have brought to the people who live around airports today. The Princesses could carry more than 300 passengers at high altitude at a speed of 385 mph, quite capable of a non-stop link between the Thames and the Hudson River at New York. But in 1952 BOAC drew the line under its flying boat operations and the prototypes were laid up forlornly on Calshot Spit. The great hangars of the days of RAF occupation now house Hampshire County Council's Activities Centre, where there are courses on everything from rock climbing to fencing. Just inshore of them, some terraces of red-brick houses, once the quarters of the Calshot personnel, were pressed into service in the early Sixties as accommodation for refugees from the island of Tristan da Cunha, which was evacuated when it was threatened by a volcanic eruption. Being dumped in a hectic and noisy environment after the peace of their island was a bit of a jolt for the islanders. Significantly, they lost no time in going back home when the island was pronounced safe.

Across the saltings outside Eling harbour tall pylons stride as if indifferent to the terrain to link Marchwood power station with the grid. The view eastward from Eling would hardly have Isaac Watts in raptures, with a mile-long industrial estate on the shore side of the reclaimed container berth. The railway line to Bournemouth swings west and crosses the Test here, on a bridge which almost touches the surface of the water at high spring tides. It is not quite the barrier to exploration upstream that it appears because beyond the railway and the concrete roadbridge parallel to it, the river disintegrates into a skein of small streams hidden among tall reeds. Venturesome canoeists explore farther, but for larger craft the railway bridge at Redbridge is the limit to navigation. In the days when railways used wooden sleepers instead of concrete ones, there used to be a works here where the pine sleepers, imported from Russia or Scandinavia, would be delivered by barge from Southampton Docks to be pickled in preservatives ready for use.

The old part of Redbridge, a comparatively attractive village street which used to carry westbound traffic, is hidden behind the new fast road and its flyovers. The original road bridge is still there, a squat 17th century structure which even by the early 1930s had no hope of coping with the increase in motor traffic. So the new bridge, vaunted as quite an ambitious structure in its day, was built beside it. It was extensively modified in the early Eighties with flyovers, extra lanes and whatnot. And already it barely copes with the enormous flood of heavy lorries, buses and cars that funnel over it ceaselessly.

When in the 1960s the writing was on the wall for passenger liners, their trade already being whittled by transatlantic airliners, the Docks chiefs planned to cater for another seaborne traffic, cargoes by container. The new container berth at the western end of the Docks was built, dredged and soon in business. Ironically, the long, straight Western Docks quay which the container ships have to pass to reach the new terminal is now largely unused. With hindsight it is easy, perhaps, to suggest that conversion there, instead of starting from scratch at Millbrook, might have done just as well. As well as containers, Southampton is establishing itself as a specialist port for handling grain.

Near Dock Head, which juts out at the confluence of the Itchen and Test from the old part of the city, tall drum-like grain elevators now stand close to the site of the Ocean Terminal which in its brief day had the glamour of a cross between Heathrow and Victoria Station – anybody who was anybody was to be seen, coming or going. The Docks were well used to grain imports: cargoes were discharged directly into the large red-brick Rank's mill in the Western Docks. But the bulk export business was something new, and while there was talk elsewhere about the overproduction of cereals, Southampton Docks were building up a lucrative trade. The two silos came into use at an uncertain time for the Docks, when a long strike had made its future uncertain. But by late 1984 both installations were being used at full capacity. During one four-day loading operation 1,720 lorries arrived at once, to discharge 19,500 tons of grain, and Southampton's pigeons and sparrows had a heavenly if hazardous time, gleaning the spillage. In one week in October 1984 about 60,000 tons were exported, about half of this to the Soviet Union. As well as wheat, barley and animal feeds, the silos can also handle pulses; one of them, after a quick modification to the loading gear for the different type of cargo, handled its first consignment of peas, 2,800 tons, in September 1986.

To older Sotonians who look back on its shipping heyday (The Gateway to the Empire, or later the Commonwealth, the signs on the edge of town used to announce proudly), the demise of the regular liner traffic to the United States, South America and the Far East knocked the spirit out of Dockland. Perhaps it is as well to get changing times into context, though. After all, the passenger liner tradition here was little over a century old, shorter than Liverpool's. For a few centuries before that it had been an out-of-the-way coasting port, with the natural advantage of its double high tide (the second, a few inches lower, returns about two hours after the first) underexploited. Even as late as the 1870s Southampton was fighting for its trade. One of its strong competitors for the transatlantic trade was Plymouth, which offered not dockside facilities but a service by tender to the shore, where passengers could board fast trains to London long before the ship could reach Southampton. And of course there was Liverpool, which could look on Southampton as something of an upstart in the competition to attract passengers.

Two large liners which still remain loyal to the port are the *QE II* and the *Canberra*. Both served in the Falklands War, but the *Canberra* in particular became something of a mascot to the troops who travelled south in her. The 'Great White Whale', as she was called, was in the thick of the fighting in San Carlos Water, miraculously unharmed despite her white paint which made her as conspicuous as the Taj Mahal. On a sunny Sunday morning in 1984 the *Canberra* came home to the biggest welcome Southampton has given to a ship. Even before she entered the Solent she was surrounded by dozens of small craft, which grew to hundreds, then thousands, the closer she got to her berth in the Western Docks. The poignant thing about her that day was the streaks of brown rust down her usually immaculate topsides. She wore them that day like battle honours.

Two miles down Southampton Water from Dock Head, a solitary domed tower of red brick faced with white stone can be seen above the trees of an extensive parkland. This is the chapel and central tower, all that remains of the Royal Victoria Military Hospital, built in the Victorian

Italianate style and then a quarter of a mile long, set back about a hundred yards from the shore. The place was built in 1856–7 at a cost of £350,000, in the surge of solicitude for the soldiers of the Crimea which Florence Nightingale had awoken (she lies buried about ten miles away, just outside Romsey). It survived to minister to wounded soldiers of both world wars. Originally there was a short pier into Southampton Water to receive wounded men discharged from hospital ships anchored off. But by the later part of the First World War they were discharged at Southampton and brought by train to the hospital's own siding off the line to Portsmouth. The extensive grounds, which might have been a heaven-sent place of fresh air and peace for convalescent men, is now the Royal Victoria Country Park.

Just to the northwest along the shore is a grey stone, castellated building close to the water, often mistaken for Netley Abbey. It is Netley Castle, or rather mock-castle, built on the site of another of Henry VIII's forts and now a convalescent home.

Netley Castle

The abbey itself, a glorious ruin set romantically among trees, is out of sight from the water, back from the Netley to Woolston coast road in a sheltered dell. From the road, more trees frame a view of the water at the foot of a gently sloping belt of green. Netley Abbey stands as remote as any ancient monument on the doorstep of a great city could have the good luck to be.

Netley's main street, despite the lack of quaintness of the buildings on its landward side, is made exceptional by that tree-screened view of the water opposite. The little place even had its own cinema until the days of telly and bingo. When the hospital was in business, Netley was more of an Army village than one devoted to fishing and small boats, and a familiar sight along the street used to be convalescent soldiers in their pale-blue hospital uniforms making their first forays into the outside world, and maybe discovering with approval that Netley had a good selection of pubs. Inland, the newer parts of the village have nothing interesting to compare with this pleasant, unpretentious seafront.

In earlier times, however, Netley Abbey had much to do with the sea and sailors. In the 14th century it petitioned for the right to increase its revenues, explaining that one of the chief causes of its shortage of money was the frequent comings and goings of sailors, who made continuous demands on the hospitality of the house. In 1338, men garrisoned to guard the approaches to Southampton against the marauding French soon outstayed their welcome by stealing the abbey's sheep on foraging raids. Netley was a Cistercian house, occupied by a colony of monks from Beaulieu after its foundation by Henry III in 1239. Over at Quarr, on the Isle of Wight, there were Cistercians also, and both houses maintained a light for the guidance of shipping – one of the things noted with favour by Henry VIII's commissioners in 1536, when they gave Netley a remarkably good report for its religious discipline and the relief and comfort it afforded to lay people. But this cut no ice with Henry and his avaricious courtiers, on the lookout for a nice abbey as the basis for a country home, or the income from its estates. Good or bad, Netley had to go, and it fell like a plum into the hands of Sir William Paulet, the first Marquis of Winchester, who was Comptroller of the Royal Household. He turned the place into a residence, which apparently did not last. By the 18th century it was a ruin and sharp-eyed builders from Southampton were showing an interest in all that wealth of first-class building stone. One of these was a man named Taylor, who bought the fabric with the intention of demolishing it entirely. But while he was directing the removal of the west end of what survived of the church, the window tracery fell on him. Fellow builders, whether they saw this as the wrath of God or not, decided not to follow the late Taylor's example, and the ruin escaped further vandalism. Today the walls, set off by groomed lawns, are under the care of the Department of the Environment.

8 Southampton

To Southampton people who remember the ocean liners which used to bring such prestige and good business to the town, the great days might be said to have ended in the late 1960s with the final departure of the *Queens*, *Mary* and *Elizabeth*, to be followed in a few dismal years by nearly all the proud ships whose comings and goings had for decades seemed such a part of a well regulated world. By then the airliner had won. People had settled for a few hours of moderate discomfort to get to the far side of the world rather than devote best part of a week travelling in the world's finest hotels to New York, or for longer periods to South Africa, the Far East and Australia. Plastic food on plastic trays took the place of cuisine of Edwardian luxury, and frustrating waits in airport departure lounges rendered the dignified transfer to the liner at the quayside direct from the Ocean Liner Express from Waterloo a time-consuming obsolescence. But progress is not always logical.

In fact, the age of the liners, which was really not all that long, was only another of the city's prosperous times. The previous ones had been quite different, based not so much on the port's capacity to handle big ships as on precisely the lack of it. In the mid-18th century Southampton was devoted to the pursuit of pleasure, with assembly rooms, spas and beautiful vistas to appeal to the followers of the new cult of the picturesque. Until the time of the French wars from 1793, Southampton might have been Bath without the terraces, and could have inspired the settings for scenes from any of Jane Austen's novels. Which was appropriate, for the author had spent some time here: she lived in Southampton from the autumn of 1806 to the spring of 1809, had been at school there briefly and had danced at a public ball when she was eighteen. The Austen family had lodgings in Castle Place which, before the great shallow bay to the west of the town was reclaimed for the building of the Western Docks in the early 1930s, offered views from the top of the medieval town walls to the outskirts of the New Forest on the far side of the estuary of the River Test. In the spirit of 18th century things Gothick, it had a castle, a castellated conceit built by the second Marquess of Lansdowne. If the Austen family home had any disadvantages, it was its breezy situation, but socially there were rewards from a Southampton address.

Jane is known to have visited Netley, a few miles down Southampton Water, in a boat excursion which was called a water party. The journey, made in the company of genteel persons, ended at the romantic ruins of the abbey, then a place high on the list of things to see for every devotee of the picturesque. A theatre had been opened in French Street, which runs down to the waterfront to the westward and parallel with High Street. In its spa heyday, Southampton attracted travelling companies and the actress and tragedienne Mrs Sarah Siddons liked it enough to take residence in the town in the early 19th century, owning a house a short distance north of the Bargate.

The spa, a chalybeate spring yielding waters impregnated with iron salts, stood nearby, and is still remembered in the name of Spa Road, a narrow passageway running beside the offices of Southampton's evening paper, the *Southern Evening Echo*. Royal patronage gave it a great boost when, in 1750, Frederick, Prince of Wales, was persuaded to take the waters while on a visit to the New Forest. He also indulged in sea bathing for good measure and enthusiastically reported his enjoyment of both. Southampton was set for success. Then there was Mr Martin's Longroom, which stood just outside the town walls with views down the length of Southampton Water, and which, although run on respectable lines, catered also for gentlemen whose interest was in taking waters of another kind. Balls were held there during the summer season, and in the 1790s, when a Mr Haynes took over as Master of Ceremonies, he printed a set of rules which his patrons were expected to obey, including the injunction that 'Gentlemen are not to appear in the rooms in boots on Tuesday, Thursday and Saturday evenings' (the nights of balls) and that 'No tea table is to be carried into the card room on ball nights'.

But it was for its beautiful setting that Southampton town attracted as many visitors as did the pleasure rooms and bathing places. William Gilpin, the Vicar of Boldre, a village in the New Forest near Lymington, described the prospect of the town from the west side of the Test which, sadly, is today hidden by Docks extensions, land reclamation and industrial estates. 'Southampton Bay', he wrote, 'spreads into a noble surface of water. The town runs out like a peninsula and, with its old walls and towers, makes a picturesque appearance. On the right, forming the other side of the bay, appear the skirts of the New Forest and the opening in front is filled with a distant view of the Isle of Wight.' Such was the view in 1775.

Mary Russel Mitford, writing to a friend in 1810, was even more enthusiastic:

'Have you been at that lovely spot which combines all that is enchanting in wood and land and water with all that is "buxom, blythe and debonaire" in society – that charming town which is not only a watering place only because it is something better? . . . Southampton has in my eyes an attraction independent even of its scenery in the total absence of the vulgar hurry of business or the chilling apathy of fashion. It is indeed all life, all gaiety, but it has an airiness, an animation.'

The town's great glory, which in part survived until very recent years when the M27 motorway and its attendant roads carved through the landscape, was its approach by road from London. This bowled over the author of *The Guide to All the Watering and Sea-Bathing Places*, published in 1810: 'The approach from London is uncommonly striking. In fact, it is almost unparalleled in the beauty of its features for the space of two miles.' Describing the view that unfolded as the carriage or stagecoach breasted the last rise on the road from Winchester, revealing the marvellous view of Southampton and its waters at the far end of a long, shallow descent, he went on:

'At first appear an expanse of water and the distant Isle of Wight, the charming scenery of the New Forest and Southampton itself in pleasing

The Bargate

prospect. Elegant seats and rows of trees nearer the town line the road on both sides, and on entering the place by one of its fashionable streets, through that venerable remain of antiquity, the Bargate, gives a finish to the scene and fixes the impression of the objects through which we have passed.'

And there are other writings in the same vein, about a gracious prospect which survived until the 1830s when work began on building the Docks which were to make Southampton the premier passenger port of Britain. Looking back, through rose-tinted glasses perhaps, it seems as much was lost as was gained. By 1840 Southampton was linked to London by railway, which ended in style at the handsome Italianate station designed by Sir William Tite and which has only recently been rescued from shameful decrepitude and is being restored, although no longer as a station. Southampton Council has made commendable efforts to prevent the Dockland area of the town from becoming a rundown area with the demise of the Docks. Several of the area's good-looking Victorian terraces of town houses have been or are being restored; linking the old with the new are the Hall of Aviation, a new museum built to house a collection of aircraft which have Southampton or Solent associations – for the area's part in the development of aviation is a story in itself. Buildings, many of them dating from medieval times when Southampton was a port with a brisk trade in wine imports and wool exports, have been taken in hand and restored as accurately as possible. The old Wool House, a squat stone building overlooking the Town Quay, is at present the Maritime Museum in which models of its fishing and trading craft share the space with those of its greatest liners. Scratched into the great timbers of the interior are the names of some of the French prisoners of war whose gaol this was during the Napoleonic Wars. The distant past is still potent in Southampton.

There are several encouraging signs that despite the rundown in the Docks, the city is by no means turning away from the sea. Yachts may not be individually as important as ocean liners, but building them and supplying their needs has always been a source of employment in Southampton. Before the land along the western shore was reclaimed for the Docks, small boat yards lined Gilpin's 'Southampton Bay'. The most famous of them, and which lasted until the First War, was Pickett's yard off the Esplanade, just opposite the West Gate through which, the commemorative plate on its wall recalls, soldiers of Henry V's time marched out to embark for France and Agincourt. At Pickett's, Victorian yachtsmen now regarded as classic authors – E.F. Knight, R.C. Leslie and Erskine Childers – kept boats at various times. Only 100 yards or so from where the tide lapped the shore at Picketts is the Mayflower Park, the scene of Southampton's greatest exhibition success, its International Boat Show. This began in 1969 with just 35 exhibitors. By the early Eighties exhibitors were booking space in their hundreds and visitors were attend-

The 14ft 'Bream' in Southampton maritime museum

ing in tens of thousands. Southampton's secret of Boat Show success is its marina, built specially for the week-long duration of the show, at which yachts can lie afloat for a better appraisal by buyers, who can step aboard readily and take a trial sail down Southampton Water at the drop of a mooring warp. The show has created a successful allied event, out of town at Bursledon on the Portsmouth road where Moody's, the biggest boatyard on the Hamble River, stages a Used Boat Show during the week of the show on Mayflower Park.

THIS IMPORTANT WESTGATE LED DIRECTLY TO THE WESTQUAY WHICH FOR MANY CENTURIES WAS THE ONLY COMMERCIAL QUAY WHICH THE TOWN POSSESSED. THE GROOVES OF THE PORTCULLIS GATES AND THE APERTURES THROUGH WHICH THE DEFENDERS OF THE TOWN COULD HARASS ATTACKERS MAY STILL BE SEEN □ □ THROUGH THIS ARCHWAY MARCHED SOME OF THE ARMY OF HENRY V ON THEIR WAY TO AGINCOURT IN 1415
□ □
THE PILGRIM FATHERS EMBARKED HERE FROM THE WEST QUAY ON THE MAYFLOWER AUGUST 15TH 1620

West Gate

The demise of the Eastern Docks has seen the birth of a new entertainment and leisure centre with a nautical theme called the Ocean Village, begun in 1983 as the start of a five year plan to develop 70 acres. A mile or so up the River Itchen on the east side of the city the Northam yacht building yard of Camper & Nicholson has been redeveloped; a marina on the river is backed by a community of shops and enterprises ashore, with a slightly bohemian air about it which brightens up a drab part of the city.

All these new activities are close to the water and repaying Southampton people with the price they had to pay for the spread of the Docks – a sad lack of places to walk and take their leisure beside the water without going beyond the city boundaries to places like Weston shore near Netley, or Hythe, or Eling. The cheerful unsophistication of Southampton's own little seaside resort, the foreshore at Millbrook which disappeared under the reclamation of the 1930s, will never return. People demand their pleasures more organised today. But the waterfront is being enjoyed and that, short of making commercial use of it, seems not a bad idea.

Major excavations of the oldest part of Southampton, the Saxon port of Hamwyh on the Itchen, has revealed that in pre-Norman times the area was enjoying the earliest of its maritime booms. A later trade is recalled in the church of a small village well away from the sea to the north of the city, near Eastleigh, beside the same River Itchen but beyond the reach of salt water.

Ocean Village

Set in the floor of the church of St Nicholas at North Stoneham is a slab of bluish-grey Belgian stone, some eight feet by four, bearing in Latin an inscription which in translation states that it is 'the tomb of the Sclavonians, AD 1491'. They were a seafaring race from Dalmatia, then ruled by Venice, and seem to have been held in high regard as muscular types who provided the oar power for the Venetian galleys which traded with Southampton. They were free men, not slaves, and were proud of their calling; they even had their own trade guild. The Venetians began trading with Southampton after running into ill-feeling in the London River, probably inspired by jealousy of some sort. Perhaps they preferred to keep to themselves, which is not always popular. They seem to have followed that practice in Southampton by choosing an isolated country church for the burial of their shipmates who had died, or who met with fatal accidents, on English soil. Today the carved stone that marks their communal grave is protected from the wear of worshippers' feet by a carpet.

There is a belief that the Sclavonians' interest in North Stoneham was more practical than choosing it as their resting place. Some say they had a hand in building the church, which may explain its dedication to the patron saint of sailors.

The most eye-catching addition to the Southampton skyline in recent years is the soaring curve of the Itchen Bridge spanning the river from Southampton to Woolston. It was opened in 1977, closing after years of debate and setback the last link in the city's road transport system. In the shadow of the tall structure on the Woolston side lies Itchen Ferry, a self-explanatory name for the little waterside community from where, in past

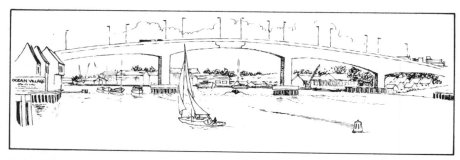

Itchen Bridge

centuries, the way to Southampton was a rowing boat, with the alternative of a long detour to a bridge upstream.

For some 140 years before the concrete curved against the sky, the famous Floating Bridge crossed; steam-powered ferries held on course by cables of chains running from bank to bank through enormous sheaves on the ferries' hulls. These faithful craft, which added a bit of adventure to a river crossing (except for commuters who had to do it twice daily in all weathers), gave a little thrill of excitement to small-boat people venturing upstream on the Itchen for the first time. Especially when running briskly before a breeze, with the gap between two crossing ferries narrowing and with those cables lifted close to the surface like some sort of boom defence

Tall ships in Southampton

until the ferries had cleared the middle of the stream. Until the last few years of the service, the floating bridges were steam powered and watching their brightly polished moving parts in action was one of the popular diversions of the crossing. When these engines were pensioned off (one of them is now in the city's Maritime Museum on the Town Quay) the Corporation Transport Department replaced them with old bus engines, which had to roar and whine to do what the venerable steam engines did with barely a hiss.

The new bridge is not only satisfying to look at from river level, it's also nice and high, which is not the most common virtue of bridges built over rivers. Owners of tall yachts passing upstream to the Shamrock Quay marina berths a few hundred yards farther on can do so without craning anxiously to watch their mastheads clear the spans.

Before the 19th century Docks were built, the Town Quay, now a broad esplanade packed with traffic on the southern side of the old walled town, used to handle Southampton's cargo traffic. Extending out from the Quay, and close by the handsome brick and stone building which used to be the headquarters of Southampton Harbour Board, is a long jetty, used until their demise by the motor barges supplying the Isle of Wight. Now there are plans to turn this oldest corner of Southampton Dockland into its newest marina, with this jetty providing access to the floating pontoons. One shipping link with the old Town Quay will remain: it will still be the terminal for the passenger ferry from Hythe.

Above Bursledon Bridge

9   Hamble to Gosport

THE RIVER Hamble is still a very pretty waterway. This needs to be said, because it is likely that of all the thousands of people who own boats moored or berthed on the river, few have taken the time to explore it intimately, knowing only the crowded fairway that leads from their mooring to the Spit Buoy at the junction with Southampton Water. Fortunately only a few of that number are ever on the move at one time, otherwise the three miles upstream to the bridges at Bursledon would be gripped in a monumental traffic jam. Boats, marinas and boatyards seem the order of things, but in that ever-handy dinghy it is worth delving inshore of the moorings lining the fairway, where patches of woodland and saltmarsh show traces of a much older river. Upstream of Hamble village and Port Hamble Marina there is the quiet, damp stretch of Satchell Marsh. Farther up on the same side there are the creeks and islets of Lincegrove and Hackett Marshes which, screened from Bursledon and Hamble airfield by the railway embankment and Badnam Copse respectively, presents a spot strangely remote from all the modern yacht traffic. On the far shore, above intermittent stretches of a low, broken dyke, stretches of broad pony pasture slope upward from the foreshore, and the rise is crowned by the woods at Holly Hill.

Both Hamble and Warsash present pleasant, unobtrusive faces to the river, and upstream from Warsash there is nothing much in the way of waterside buildings except for the sheds of Universal Shipyards, until Moody's yard at Lower Swanwick. So all is not lost on the river which bears the largest concentration of yachts and small craft in the British Isles. At last the error of the optimistic philosophy of 'room for just a few

The Jolly Sailor at Swanwick

more moorings upstream' is being heeded. But it is reasonable to assume that visitors who make a journey up the Hamble on the flood and, if it is to be a quick visit, down on the ebb, have come to see the variety of craft which make this their home base. And for anybody interested in boats, from hi-tech moderns to varnished classics, from round-the-world racing maxis to venerable one-design racers which have grown old gracefully, then the Hamble is the greatest permanent boat show on earth.

Keen explorers might care to push on upstream, squeezing gingerly past the berthing pontoons each side of the A27 road bridge at Bursledon, to the lovely riverside scenery waiting above the northernmost of Bursledon's three bridges, that carrying the M27. From here in a very small boat one can venture as far inland as the little town of Botley, famous for its flour mill, village square and one-time resident William Cobbett. And for those who time their tides and opening time equally well, there is the chance of a refreshing stop on the way at the tiny hamlet of Curbridge. Its pub, the Horse and Jockey, stands a few paces from the tree-lined river bank.

To reach these pastoral delights one has to run a narrow gauntlet between moorings and pontoons which barely gives passing space above and below the Bursledon road bridge. Upstream, where the Southampton to Portsmouth railway line crosses the river at an angle, used to be the Hamble's Slough of Despond, a repository of all sorts of abandoned wrecks and junk, just where most people viewed the river when crossing it by road or rail. Lately somebody has done a good job in tidying up the mess; wrecks have been dragged away and saltgrasses are growing over the scarred patches. Upstream of the railway bridge is a small community of moorings, the owners of the boats that lie on them obviously having no aspirations to be numbered among the Howard's Way set. But I will put in a plea to the Powers to think carefully about allowing more moorings to be sited north of the motorway bridge, intruding into what is the most unspoiled stretch of river landscape in the Solent. The river from the bridges towards Botley deserves to be left as the domain of canoeists and dinghy sailors, who have little in common with the big-yacht comings and goings downstream. At low water the channel reduces to a trickle, which curbs its potential for large-boat moorings. But why, just for once, have any at all? Many a Solent river and harbour has paid the price in losing its scenic attractiveness for the optimistic philosophy that there is always room for a few more moorings upstream. But the Hamble upstream of Bursledon pleads a special case. Downstream of the bridges, the river is a yachting base, where craft have been built and served since way back. Upstream it never has, and with the Solent's furthest reaches so sadly bereft of quiet corners, never needs to be.

From the mouth of the river below Warsash begins what Barry Shurlock has aptly named the Long Beach. And long it is: the gravelly foreshore runs all the way southeast to Gilkicker Point, at the southern tip of Gosport, and nearly all of that bracing, breezy shoreline is accessible to walkers. Well-shod ones, that is. This marathon stretch forms one of the finest parts of the Hampshire County Council's long-distance footpath, called the Solent Way, which runs either along the North Solent shore or as close to it as possible, from the county boundary at Emsworth westward to Hurst Castle. For those who lack the stamina for the whole thing, the Long Beach stretch is a recommended way of doing some dry-land pilotage of the lower Hamble, Southampton Water and the central part of the Solent.

Along here can be found some of the most pleasant coastal scenery east of Southampton Water, contrasting the lush meadowlands bordering the River Meon on its last miles to the sea at Titchfield Haven to the shingle banks of Browndown, where in season the yellow of the gorse sets off the purple heather and, here and there, the delicate tissue paper petals of the yellow horned poppy. Browndown Ranges is an important plant habitat; Phil Colebourn, who wrote the Hampshire County Council handbook to the wildlife of the county's coasts, describes it as:
'an unusual shingle habitat, like nowhere else in southern Britain except perhaps at Dungeness. Here a series of low parallel shingle ridges, created by storms, carries a patchy cover of silty peat with ling and gorse and occasional stunted oaks. Pebbles and bare peat carry a rich assortment of ground-living lichens.

'There is an unusual flora, too, with burnet rose, slender-flowered thistle and a plentiful population of Nottingham catchfly with its delicate

Thistle

Horned Poppy

Titchfield Haven Bird Sanctuary

drooping white flowers. The red threads of lesser dodder can also be found, parasitic on the ling and producing tiny pink flowers in summer. Further along the coast, at Gilkicker Point, another area of stable shingle has different specialities, including pale flax, pale toadflax, sheepsbit, carline thistle and the annual hare's-tail grass. These are absent at Browndown, for each of these fragile coastal habitats differs in some way from the others. Gilkicker is also a good place to find rare and uncommon coastal sedges: distant sedge, dotted sedge, long-bracted sedge and divided sedge all grow here.'

The main break in this long stretch of storm-heaped shingle is at the tiny harbour of Titchfield Haven, formed by another of those eastward-curving spits of shingle around the River Meon's entrance. This is the home of Hill Head Sailing Club (named after the clifftop village immediately to the south) and its members aver that it is the most pleasantly sited sailing club on the Solent. I can say, with no trace of impartiality, that they are right. The Haven dries completely at low water, as do the gravel flats some quarter of a mile from the shore. The size of the place means that boats of 14 to 21 feet and able to take the mud lie happiest there. Right alongside the Haven is Hampshire County Council's Titchfield Haven Nature Reserve, created out of the marshy lower reaches of the Meon and famous for its waterfowl and migrant birds. Hill Head SC has its very own dinghy class, the Jacquelines, sturdy clinker-built sloops

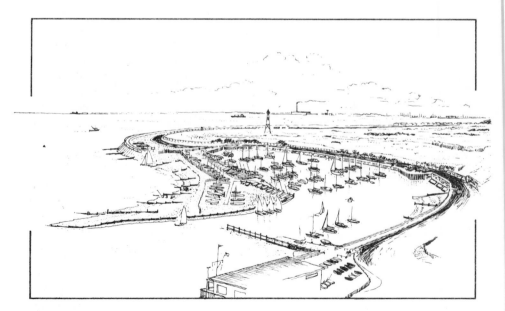

Titchfield Haven Harbour

with a pronounced raked bow, designed and built by a club founder-member, now its honorary harbourmaster and friend-in-need to all, Tommy Robertson. In other clubs, local classes have declined. Happily, the Jacquelines have not only survived the plywood and fibreglass revolutions, they are making a comeback, with starters in class racing on the increase.

Inland from the Haven there is a magnificent broad stretch of meadowland, bordered by trees for much of its 2½ mile length to Titchfield village to the north. A good footpath to the village skirts the nature reserve for its first mile, then follows the bank of a tiny disused canal right into Titchfield, with several stiles to climb over but only one minor road to cross all the way.

Where these lush pastures now feed herds of cattle, the sea used to penetrate inland as far as Titchfield, which was a small port until the 17th century when the Third Earl of Southampton, with an eye on the extra acres that could be added to his domains, built a lock at the seaward end of the Meon and a seawall to keep out the tide. He had the canal, alongside which the footpath now runs, built to provide access of a sort for boats from the Solent to Titchfield, but this was abandoned in the 1890s. This piece of land reclamation did not please the people of Titchfield: it removed, with the tidal water, an important source of livelihood. Every year the village holds a bonfire festival and it is not Guy Fawkes who is symbolically burned here, but the Earl, as thanks for his high-handed interference with the natural scheme of things.

About half a mile north of the village and across the A27 road is the ruin of Place House, as the secular rebuilding on the site of the dissolved Titchfield Abbey was named. The abbey had been founded in 1232 by Henry III as a house of Premonstratensian Canons. Its fate during the Dissolution was much the same as that of other religious houses throughout the land. The abbey buildings and lands were bought up by Thomas Wriothesley, known as the Asset Stripper, who had acquired property at Beaulieu and other places. Within days of the Canons quitting the abbey, thus ending a religious occupation of the site that had lasted for 300 years, Wriothesley was selling off the valuables to anyone who made suitable offers.

From its slightly disreputable origins, Place House (as distinct from Palace House at Beaulieu) was to be linked in its domestic phase with two men. One was William Shakespeare, whose patron was the Third Earl of Southampton, he who cut off the village from the sea. There is a popular legend that Shakespeare spent much time at Place House and that *Romeo and Juliet* was staged in the great abbey tithe barn (still there, with magnificent beams, and still a farm barn, with a popular farm shop that means it is open most days). Another more slender Shakespeare tradition in the village is that he got the name Gobbo for the character in *The*

Titchfield Abbey

Merchant of Venice from a Titchfield family. But this has been ruled out as somebody's optimistic misreading of the name Holte in a parish register.

The Bard's associations with Titchfield are therefore mainly conjectural, but 50 years after him another visitor came to Place House and his visit is well documented. As the Civil War turned fatally against King Charles I, he fled to Titchfield from Hampton Court in 1647, probably remembering the place from a royal visit there with Queen Henrietta Maria in 1625. For some reason he was persuaded that the Isle of Wight would be a safe refuge for a runaway King, and that Colonel Hammond, the Parliamentary Governor of Carisbrooke Castle, might be won round to his side. From Place House he rode to the Meon shore, along the road to somewhere near Hill Head (along the canalside footpath there is a small red-brick bridge named Hammond's Bridge, no doubt a coincidence) where he was taken by boat to the Island and eventual imprisonment. Colonel Hammond must have played a subtle game.

Today Place House is a ruin again. The Wriothesley family moved out and later owners used much of the fabric to build Cams Hall, a grand country house near Fareham. It seems fitting, after those 300 years of monastic history which came to a brutal end under Henry VIII, that the place is hardly ever referred to by local people as Place House: it is always Titchfield Abbey. Titchfield itself has managed to elude the embracing arms of sprawling Fareham advancing from the east and the conglomerate of Warsash, Park Gate and Locks Heath on the western side. But Hampshire County Council, in a less benign light this time, full of stubborn enthusiasm for its vaunted South Hampshire project, is allowing new building to get close enough to endanger the village's individuality, and the signs are in place, proudly drawing attention to 'prime prestige office sites', a grandiose business park to the north at Whiteley, and other emblems of progress.

Lee-on-Solent is still what it started life as just a century ago: a pleasant seaside residential place, notable for its enormously long seafront. At its western end there are the grey-painted hangars and other buildings of HMS *Daedalus*, the Fleet Air Arm training establishment. Hidden from the sea front is its extensive airfield. It has grown from the seaplane base established at Lee before the First World War for the Royal Flying Corps. Today, helicopter training is one of its major activities – and here a word of advice for yachtsmen passing east or west between Ryde and East Cowes: training sessions, often involving Royal Marines and helicopters, frequently take place here and they often involve choppers hovering low over the water. It pays to give them a wide berth, because the downdraft from the blades is considerable. Across the seafront road outside the main gate of *Daedalus* there is a broad concrete ramp, evidence of the establishment's past interest in seaplanes. This is still in use today. But instead of planes, it was recently Hovercraft that were launched here by the Hovercraft Trials Unit, an inter-Service organisation within the base.

The Fleet Air Arm's most famous aeroplane, the Fairey Swordfish, is honoured, if in name only, by a pub called the Swordfish standing close to the foreshore between *Daedalus* and Seafield Park, another naval training establishment just inland to the northwest.

Lee-on-Solent has, of course, a thriving sailing club, where launching a dinghy down a concrete ramp on the breeziest lee shore in the Solent is one of the skills soon learned. The club's famous home class was the Solent Seagull: the third or fourth marque to bear the name was designed by the great Charles Nicholson just after the Second World War. The Seagulls are of special interest because they are built with reversed clinker planks – the planks overlap upward instead of downward. This idea, which was aimed at increasing speed by reducing the resistance of the downward lapping planks, had been pioneered by the Fareham boatbuilder Percy See, and the value of the method was rediscovered in later years by the designers of fast powerboats. Apart from the Seagulls the idea never caught on with sailing craft, maybe because their low speeds made the reverse lap less of an advantage.

Next door to Lee SC's boat pound is that of the Elmore Angling Club, which stores a fleet of impressive size and variety. A massive bit of organisation earned a place in the *Guinness Book of Records* for the keen

Elmore men when they staged, as a fund-raising venture with the RNLI, the biggest beach-fishing competition in the country, in which they seem to have won the forebearance of bathers and other beach users and stationed competitors along the shore for miles. Lee is an attractive, not too posh, seaside residential resort, where modern blocks of flats seem less in keeping than the villas they overlook. It eluded ambitious plans to be made into a major Solent resort, although in the late 19th century it was linked by railway with Gosport. This was discontinued in the mid-1930s.

All along the north shore of the Solent are the sites of projects inspired by the popularity of the Isle of Wight during Queen Victoria's residence there, for opening up new rail-ferry links with the Island. Southeast of Lee, beyond the shingle beach behind which lies Browndown Ranges, is Stokes Bay, the seaside for Alverstoke, the affluent end of Gosport. Still surviving here are the remains of a pier which used to carry boat trains to connect with steamers for Ryde. Compared with the sheltered terminals within Portsmouth Harbour, this seems an exposed place for such an enterprise, but it worked. Services started from there in 1863 and survived until the First World War.

Standing squat and dramatic at the southeast end of the Long Beach is Gilkicker Fort, part of Palmerston's sea defence system around Portsmouth Harbour and its approaches. Unlike most of the others, Gilkicker was given a useful job after its heavy guns and mortars were removed. Because of its position, giving a splendid sight both ways along the Solent and the approaches to Spithead, it made an ideal signal station for ships to report, or 'make their number'.

Gilkicker Point would seem to be the natural place for a tide-rip, but I have never encountered one in years of pottering past the place. A look at the chart reveals that the main Solent streams flow past the point without being forced to one side or confined, in the classic way that tide races are made. The main channel to Portsmouth is about a mile eastward and on the shoals off Haslar Sea Wall the tide has nothing much in the way of strength, so there is not the turbulence of two streams colliding at Gilkicker. From the Point, the land bears sharply away northeast, past Haslar Hospital and the buildings of HMS *Dolphin*, the true home of the Navy's submarine arm. There is shallow water close to the Haslar Wall, up the long sloping sea face of which the swells that roll in from Spithead in easterly weather spend their force.

Yachts, which do not need the deep water of the main channel east of Spit Sand Fort, enjoy the convenient placing of two prominent marks to give a transit for a safe approach. These are the tall Naval War Memorial on the seafront lined up with the spire of St Jude's Church about half a mile inland in Southsea. For its last couple of cables, the deep channel runs close to and parallel with the seafront at Southsea. Ferries, warships and cargo vessels are constantly on the move here and the tiny entrance to such an important harbour demands a keen lookout and good lane discipline. Even before you arrive it offers small-boat sailors the sense of being part of a tradition. These waters, and the shores that surround them, have been at the heart of England's naval history for 700 years. The great days may have gone, but the atmosphere lingers.

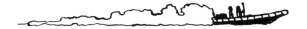

10   Portsmouth and Gosport

APPROACHING from the sea, from the Nab or from the south of the Island round Bembridge Ledge, Portsmouth at first looks like a mirage. Portsea Island as a whole is flat and low-lying and from a good way off in clear weather its taller buildings seem to float like a line of ice, now that tall tower blocks are so numerous in the city. Closer, past the Warner buoy and approaching the gateway through Horse Sand and No Man's Land Forts, the stone walls of the old fortifications gleam as bright as new concrete despite their age. There is an odd mixture of styles here in a short distance. Southsea Castle, trying to look serious and warlike despite the mock lighthouse perched on top; the wide green of Southsea Common, which is one of the finest and broadest expanses of seaside gardens anywhere around the coast; the big wheels and dippers of the funfair at Clarence Pier; then the Square and Round Towers and the Hot Walls that link them, Portsmouth's favourite grandstand for watching important nautical arrivals and departures. Many a happy homecoming has begun here, where arriving warships passing through the entrance are close enough to the walls for faces to be recognised and waves exchanged. The last sombre occasion of the departure of a fleet was in a hazy morning in 1982, when a procession of warships passed seaward on their way to the Falklands War, with sweethearts and wives standing where countless others had stood over the centuries, watching them go and thinking bravely of their return.

It is about a mile and a half from Southsea Castle to the Harbour mouth and for interest and variety the passing traffic of craft large and small is unequalled. For more than half that distance the deep fairway leading into the Harbour turns parallel with the shore so that the ships that pass are seen close to. Clarence Pier, overlooked by the funfair, is just a stump compared with the more traditionally ornate South Parade Pier beyond Southsea Castle to the east, but the Clarence used to be a busy place in the holiday months. Here thousands embarked on paddle steamer trips, across the Solent to Ryde, up Southampton Water, or on any of several routes.

Ancient and modern buildings face each other across the entrance to the Harbour, surprisingly narrow for such a large and important expanse of water. On the left side going in is the red brick of HMS *Dolphin*, the submarine base. On the right, the Hot Walls and Round Tower of the old city fortifications. Why 'Hot', people ask. One of the best guesses is that there were braziers kept here to heat shot that would have been fired against invaders and their ships. But one Portsmouth guidebook coins a modern explanation that is apt: just below the walls, on the tiny bit of shingle foreshore, is a favourite sunbathing spot for Portsmouth people. This tiny corner between the Sally Port and the Round Tower is a suntrap, where unprepared bodies soon get done a painful scarlet. The agonised owners of them would appreciate the truth behind the name.

John Scott Hughes, who was also struck by the way Southsea rises out of the horizon when seen from an approaching vessel, likened it to the Italian port of Taranto, from a distance. He hinted, too, at a friendly quality in those fortress walls fronting the harbour mouth: the Round Tower was 'massive yet likeable'. He was right. Even on a cloudy day a brief break of sunshine sets the walls gleaming with a special brightness all their own. Perhaps there is some quality in the stone of which they are built, or maybe their south-facing position gives them maximum exposure to the light.

But conning a small boat through the entrance is best done without distraction by the venerable stones. Small craft are warned by a notice to keep well to the south side of the channel, leaving the rest for the ferries, coasters and warships that pass in and out constantly. In addition to the traffic – and on a sunny weekend morning in summer yachts explode from the place like seeds blown from a dandelion clock – there is the formidable tide that runs here. When you think that an area of water of about 15 square miles has to fill and empty through a gap not much more than 200 yards wide, the force of the tides here can be appreciated. The ebb is strongest, nearly five knots at springs and more than that on big equinoctial tides. Against a southeasterly wind this rate of flow can raise a wickedly steep sea.

As well as forts and guns, the harbour mouth was until quite recently equipped with chains (later booms) which could be made fast on each side to prevent a forced entry. A small space is still called the Boom Yard, and it was probably here that John Leland, on his visit to Portsmouth in about

1540, commented on the 'mightie chayne of yron' ready to be hauled taut across the harbour if the French attempted a raid. How the technology of Tudor times coped with making and the raising/lowering of this enormous thing is a mystery. Each link in the chain was said to be four feet long and this immense weight, which lay on the seabed in readiness, had to be raised and tensioned just below the surface. Scott Hughes recalled seeing a photograph taken early this century showing a piece of the chain exposed by a severe winter gale after lying forgotten in the seabed mud. According to him, the thickness of the links was about that of the thigh of a youth posing beside it in the picture, and the end was bolted into the base of the Round Tower.

In contrast to the stone tower on the north side of the entrance is an eye-catching house with its observation tower topped by a fine gilded ship weathervane, standing right on the water's edge. This was the home for his latter years of the marine artist W. L. Wyllie, who moved here from a home beside the lower Thames where he had worked on his famous paintings and etchings of Thames and Medway sailing barges.

Wyllie had a fondness for the grimy face of seafaring. Like the French artist Millet, who portrayed the toilers of the field, he portrayed the toilers afloat, the barge skippers, the stevedores and the sailors coaling ship. And he was a good hand aboard a sailing boat. To the end of his life he raced in the International 14 foot dinghy class against such people as Uffa Fox. He

Portsmouth Sailing Club

was Commodore of Portsmouth Sailing Club, whose clubhouse is just across the narrow waterside street from his home, and one of their native classes from the early 1930s was a 10 foot clinker-built, sloop-rigged open boat which honoured him in its name, the Wyllie 10-Footer. Past the artist's house, there opens up the classic view of Old Portsmouth; the jolly jumble of waterside buildings, private houses, warehouses and pubs, with today a few tall blocks of flats added, that huddle right by the water at Point. This spot has been a favourite subject for artists since the 18th century when Rowlandson did his famous satirical view of the scene, featuring tars and their molls, which this century inspired the orchestral overture 'Portsmouth Point' by the composer Sir William Walton. Streets so narrow that you can almost touch the buildings on both sides with outstretched arms thread this tiny community. Point (old Pointers insist you never say THE Point) is respectable today, even a bit prim. But in the 18th century, at the time of Rowlandson's droll painting, this was as wicked a quarter as possessed by any sailor town, with beer houses by the dozen, gin shops and brothels all vying to relieve sailors, and the soldiers of the garrison, of their pay. The sinful delights of Point were well placed to waylay sailors because many of them came ashore after being paid off at the end of a commission at the Sally Port, just along Broad Street, instead of in the Dockyard itself.

Old merchant shipping traditions are still preserved in the Camber Dock, Portsmouth's original commercial harbour almost hidden behind the terraced houses on the north side of Broad Street. Trade here has declined in only the last few years, and yachts and small craft are taking the space where coasters and colliers used to berth. The green-painted warehouses on the quays used to be fragrant with cargoes of discharged

Camber Dock

fruit or wine shipped in bulk tanks. In the southern corner of this tiny crook-shaped basin was the Vosper Shipyard, now closed down, where fast warships were built, mostly for foreign navies. At the far end the car ferries to and from Fishbourne on the Isle of Wight squeezed into their loading ramp; and, for good measure, colliers from the North used to serve the imposing power station that dominated the Camber until its demolition only a few years ago. Visitors could wander freely here unchallenged: there were no 'keep out' signs, though a sharp lookout was needed constantly to prevent being knocked over by the mobile cranes that busied about the place, or the lorries that loaded the Camber's imports. Today the place has lost its trade to a new commercial dock complex north of the Dockyard, where the ubiquitous container has taken the fun (for spectators, that is) out of watching ships load and discharge. But the Camber is still a lively place. One of the warehouses is today occupied by a fresh fish packing depot, adding a whiff of what must have been a rich aroma around the place in the old days. Small trawlers come alongside here for maintenance and repairs to their fishing gear, and the enormous car ferries, although they have moved across the harbour to the site once occupied by the power station, still swing in the tiny basin with nonchalant panache. How so much traffic could ever be accommodated in such a small space is hard to imagine now. The simple answer is that the standard of seamanship by all involved was and is very high. Not least by the men who handled the pale blue launches of Butcher's fleet. These boats are known to Southsea holidaymakers for their round-the-Harbour trips, but there were others, well padded with rope fenders, which acted as the Camber's tugboats, squeezing and easing coasters, which looked enormous in these confined surroundings, in and out of berths. The launch fleet carried on this work at the new quays to the north, up the harbour.

The Camber is a survivor of the sort of small seaport which was virtually universal in the last century: wherever you looked there were men plying their various trades. In one corner, working in a two-storey workshop with rusty corrugated iron walls, George Feltham and his son Cecil built yachts, launches and dinghies until George's death in the early 1970s. In the matey spirit which prevailed in the Camber, Vospers, which were right next door, would lend a crane if a new boat from the Feltham shop had to be lifted on a trailer for delivery elsewhere. Facing the water at the other end of Broad Street is the sailmaking loft and chandlery of Lucas & Son, a long-established Portsmouth firm where stocks of bitumen paints, copper nails, galvanised chain reflect a trade with working and fishing boats as well as carefully groomed yachts.

And, the crowning touch, set amidst the warehouses and right on the quayside the Camber has its own pub. At the time of writing, however, there are suspicious signs that this house, once the busy refresher of dockies and seamen, is being tarted up into something more grand, now that yachts are beginning to take over more of the Camber's quay space. There are other pubs on Point, looking out across the harbour and with the wash of passing vessels almost lapping the foundations of their walls. The Still and West is a name that announces itself to every passing vessel. Another has the newer title of The Lone Sailor, named in honour of the Portsmouth greengrocer Alec Rose, who in 1968 sailed his sloop (she was rigged with a small mizzen for the voyage) *Lively Lady* around the world and back to a civic welcome at Southsea that the people of Portsmouth turned into a city holiday.

Just north of the Camber stands what was one of the Navy's most famous shore establishments, HMS *Vernon*, the underwater weapons and mine defence school. It achieved world-wide fame in its last years by offering its small deep-water basin to the yachts competing in the Whitbread Round the World Race, sailed from Portsmouth every four years, for last-minute fitting out and provisioning, and for the spectacular welcomes that mark their return. Next door is Portsmouth Harbour railway station, where passengers step directly from trains onto the Seaspeed ferries for Ryde Pier. The old stalwarts on this route, the *Shanklin* and the *Brading*, have been upstaged somewhat by the arrival of a faster, but smaller, catamaran-type craft, which received a cool reception from commuters when it was introduced recently. But it is certain that this nippy newcomer will need the sheer carrying capacity of one or more of the traditional ferries to help with the summer volume of traffic between Portsmouth and Ryde. A great sweep of road has been built on piles to the seaward end of the pier on which the Harbour station stands, curtailing the size of a small half-tidal space where inshore fishing boats moor below the Hard, and once the embarkation point for small wherries and harbour passenger craft. Overlooking the Hard is the handsome frontage of the Keppel's Head, the Naval officers' 'local', next door to another of their important calls when ashore in Portsmouth, Gieves the tailors.

The finest buildings to be seen around the shores of Portsmouth Harbour are those built for military and naval purposes. Those of the Dockyard, some going back to the days of Queen Anne, are of such architectural value that, as the Dockyard contracts, they will become the centre of an extensive museum complex surrounding the drydock where HMS *Victory* lies. Until the early 1980s she was the most visited historic ship in Britain. But then another, even older but more ravaged by time, was raised from the waters off Spitsand by giant cranes, watched by thousands from a ring of spectator boats and by millions more on television. Even when the remains of the *Mary Rose's* hull were lifted from the water after years of careful preparatory work by amateur divers, the excitement among archaeologists and marine historians at the achievement was nothing compared to that over the detailed examination of the objects that were found preserved in the silt among her timbers, both before and after raising them. The hull itself offered enough of its structure intact to show the sort of shipbuilding techniques used around the time Europeans were discovering America and the sea routes to the Indies; much of this study was carried out underwater, before she was lifted. But there was much more than that. 'A perfect time capsule showing life in Tudor times' was how she was described, when the mud of centuries was gently washed away, producing amazing finds: plums and raisins from the ship's stores, fleas from the sailors' clothes, and one of the most vivid links yet one of the most commonplace – a leaf that may have blown aboard as the *Mary Rose* lay alongside in Portsmouth Harbour. She was named after Henry VIII's favourite sister in 1509. In 1545, watched by Henry and his court, she sailed with other ships to engage a French force sighted approaching the Isle of Wight. What went wrong is unclear, but it seems that her lower gunports were not properly secured – some statements cast aspersions on the sobriety of her crew – and she heeled in a breeze and quickly took water aboard and sank, with the loss of her entire crew and captain, Sir George Carew. Those remains of the sailors which were brought ashore when the wreck was raised were later accorded a burial service, using the form of service which would have been customary in their own day.

Even with that staggering death toll, the *Mary Rose* was not the greatest Solent shipping disaster. In August 1782 the *Royal George*, a sister ship of HMS *Victory*, was lying at anchor undergoing minor repairs. To get at a part of her hull below the waterline, ballast and guns were shifted across to careen her. It was routine and hardly anybody gave it a thought. Wives and children of sailors were visitors aboard. There was a loud crack, underwater timbers, probably grievously rotten, gave way and she sank in the space of a couple of minutes, taking with her 900 of the estimated 1,200 people on board.

The gilding and paint is kept bright aboard HMS *Victory*, as befits the chief treasure of the Navy. For years no such favoured treatment was devoted to a smaller, humbler but not much younger vessel lying afloat in the Harbour within sight of *Victory*'s soaring spars. She was the frigate *Foudroyant*, built in Bombay in 1817 as HMS *Trincomalee*. Until recently it seemed that a dismal end was in store for this, the oldest warship still afloat. She was run by the Foudroyant Trust which did a good job in giving youngsters, boys and girls, a chance to live aboard for a holiday, to learn boat handling and seamanship and to sling their hammocks at bedtime just like real old salts.

In a long and courageous struggle against decay, the Trust launched various projects, like selling some of the iron cannon she had stowed in her hold as ballast. She made a few journeys under gentle tow to Husbands Shipyard at Southampton for what first-aid repairs to her hull could be met.

She had been built of teak, which is why she had lasted so long. But rain, frost and humidity, rather than seawater, will destroy the hardest wood and it seemed that the *Foudroyant* was to become the spectre at the feast in Portsmouth's ambition to become a major ship museum. Then in 1987 things suddenly looked up. The Victorian ironclad, HMS *Warrior*, beautifully restored at Hartlepool over seven years at a cost of £6 million, made an entrance into Portsmouth harbour worthy of a grand dame of an interesting age (She was built at Blackwall on the Thames in 1860).

Within days it seemed that everything had been organised for two more patients to be on their way for the Hartlepool treatment. Floated side by side on a submersible barge were a first world war vessel and the *Foudroyant*. When she returns eventually in her restored glory she will deserve a *Warrior*-style welcome from the Solent's small-boat community.

As for the sailors who manned the ships, their truest memorial remains Point. Why here, and not in the Dockyard half a mile away? Because it was through the Sally Port in Broad Street, still used by visitors going for a breezy walk along the Hot Walls, that sailors joined their ships when they had been worked out from the Dockyard to the anchorage at Spithead. As the sign over the gateway says to this day, 'heroes innumerable' embarked here to fight their country's battles. And of those innumerable heroes, many of the officers had by the time of the Napoleonic Wars set up house in Portsmouth. Jane Austen, who knew Southampton better than Portsmouth, but had family connections with the Navy, described the domestic side of the sea officer's life in *Mansfield Park*. At that time Southampton was several rungs up the ladder above Portsmouth in terms of gentility. Fanny Price, in *Mansfield Park*, coming to Portsmouth from the country, found the place noisy, dirty and smelly. But the Georgians seem to have been incapable of ugly building, and as there were pleasant surrounding areas away from the low life of Point, the town must have had town houses of a quality to attract naval officers and their families. Of all the towns in which Jane Austen's novels or characters are set, Portsmouth is the only one not of the 'genteel' sort which she describes in some detail. She may not have cared much for the activities in the dingier parts of the town and around the Dockyard Gate, but she like so many others, was captivated by the effect, seemingly unique to Portsmouth, of the special sparkle of light that reflects off its white walls and off the water below on a breezy sunny day. As her biographer Maggie Lane has pointed out, not only was Jane the sister of a naval officer, but as her travels indicate she loved being by the sea, which helps to explain this vivid passage, describing a walk by Fanny Price along the ramparts:

'The day was uncommonly lovely. It was really March, but it was April in its mild air, brisk soft wind and bright sun, occasionally clouded for a minute; and everything looked so beautiful under the influence of such a sky, the effects of the shadows pursuing each other, on the ships in

Spithead and the island beyond, with the ever-varying hues of the sea now at high water, dancing in its glee and dashing against the ramparts with so fine a sound . . .'

A perfect description, still as valid as when she wrote it. Over the Sally Port gate is a gilt bust of Charles I, which commemorates his safe landing there on October 5, 1623 after travels abroad with the Duke of Buckingham, one of the purposes of which was to find a suitable bride. Actually the bust is not the original stone one, which was becoming badly ravaged by the weather and was removed to Portsmouth Museum. The bust in the niche now is a replica, made of fibreglass. It looks splendid, and will no doubt maintain its looks better than the stone original. Maybe the Duke of Buckingham reflected on that happy return three years later, when in August 1628 he was superintending the last-minute preparations for his projected expedition to La Rochelle, on the French Atlantic coast, as a gesture of support for the Huguenots, hard-pressed by Cardinal Richelieu. He was using the house of a friend in High Street as his headquarters and about to leave it, having said farewell to his wife and sister, when a young subaltern, John Felton, burst forward and stabbed the King's favourite in the breast. Felton was a Puritan, and said that he did the deed to 'rid the Commonwealth of a monster'. He was executed for the murder at Tyburn and his remains were brought back to Portsmouth to hang on a gibbet on the beach at Southsea, near the site of the present Clarence Pier. The episode, in romanticised form, was worked into the novel *The Three Musketeers* by Alexandre Dumas in 1844.

Many in Stuart England might have agreed with Felton's description of Buckingham as a monster, the self-willed and virtually all-powerful favourite of the King. But if the populace shed no tears for George Villiers, Duke of Buckingham, they flowed early on the morning of September 14, 1805, a few paces from the scene of the Buckingham murder. Here stood the George Hotel and it was here that Nelson, on his way to join the fleet off Cadiz by frigate, spent his last night on English, or indeed any, soil. From the George to the Sally Port, visible at the end of Broad Street, is only some 200 yards. Such a crowd had gathered that Nelson had to make a detour, but he was discovered and cheered all the way to his waiting barge.

So many interesting buildings were lost during the prolonged blitz on Portsmouth during the Second World War, but the loss of the George Hotel was particularly sad. It would have well qualified for some sort of 'heroes innumerable stayed here' plaque over the door. Today it is remembered by an inscribed stone set in the wall of a block of low-rise flats on the site. As for the Duke of Buckingham, he has achieved somewhat gaudy immortality by a pub sign across the street, done in bright colours.

Portsmouth Dockyard looks thoroughly Georgian in its architecture, with some Victorian additions. All the building has a confident sense of permanence – not shared by most of the work put up in Portsmouth at large to replace the immense amount of destruction done by the Luftwaffe in the war. The doings of the 18th century Royal Navy now contend for the title of England's national epic, and the fine red brick buildings within the Dockyard gates help to preserve the image. But the Romans were first to have an eye to the Harbour's possibilities as a naval base, only their choice of a site was to the north, at Portchester.

The value of drydocks, into which a ship could be floated and the water then pumped out to allow work to her bottom, has been well known to seamen since ships became too big to beach or careen for a quick repair. It was not the idea that was lacking, but the technology to put it into effect. In 1194, in the reign of Richard Coeur de Lion, the first attempt was made to dig a drydock for the King's ships. It was near the site of Vernon Creek and was merely a hole dug in the mud which the tides soon washed away. By 1495, when Henry VII ordered a more thorough job, Robert Brygandine, the Clerk of the Ships, built a basin lined with timber and stone. But there were no gates: once a vessel was floated in, a small army of men had to start work closing the end with stones and clay. The job probably took much longer than the repairs to the ship inside. Then the water inside had to be removed with hand pumps, grinding labour that was only done away with with the invention of steam-powered pumps.

The first vessel known to have been built at Portsmouth for use as a warship was the *Sweepstake* in 1497. The second was rather better remembered, the *Mary Rose*. She was launched in 1509, the year of Henry VIII's accession and was rebuilt in 1536, nine years before she capsized in the East Solent. After the Tudor beginnings Portsmouth's output of ships for the Navy was continuous. One of the newest in the line of battle at Trafalgar was the *Dreadnought*, completed just four years previously. The Dockyard used all the advanced technologies of succeeding generations, from sail to steam, wood to iron, steam to oil and iron to steel. In 1905 the Dockyard sprang a surprise on the rest of the major navies by building a later *Dreadnought*, the first all-big-gun man-of-war, in just a year and a day.

This record time for building a battleship was never broken. *Dreadnought* was new in many ways. The hull freeboard was high, to keep her dry at sea. Her ten 12-inch guns were intended to allow her to fight at long range and at high speed. She was the first battleship to be fitted with turbines instead of reciprocating engines, and her four screws gave her a then uncatchable speed of 21 knots. She was built with coal boilers but designed so that she could switch to oil-firing without major refitting. The irony of this revolutionary vessel was that she allowed rival navies to copy the concept at once, which they duly began to do, so that the Royal Navy's stunning surprise was soon absorbed in another arms race, with everybody again equal. By the time of the First World War *Dreadnought* had been overtaken by design improvements. She served with the Grand Fleet during the war, but her moment of glory came in 1915 when she sighted and rammed the U-boat which had torpedoed the British cruisers *Hogue, Abukir* and *Cressy* soon after war had broken out. She was broken up in 1923.

The story ended in 1967 when HMS *Andromeda*, laid down the previous year, became the last warship to be built at Portsmouth. She was a Leander Class frigate and in May 1982 sailed from Plymouth to form part of HMS *Invincible's* close escort to the Falklands. In June of that year *Andromeda* led HMS *Cardiff* and the liner *Canberra* into Port Stanley after the Argentine surrender. By the mid-1980s she and *Sirius*, another Leander Class frigate, were the only two Portsmouth-built warships left in service.

In the 1960s the Navy's traditional primacy in Portsmouth Harbour began to change. North of the Dockyard, between it and Whale Island, Portsmouth city embarked on a major venture of building a commercial port from scratch. The Albert Johnson Quay, named after one of the city's most visionary fathers, was opened in 1967 to serve coasters and containers, and was soon followed by other facilities including cross-Channel ferry berths. All these have succeeded beyond most experts' hopes. Portsmouth, indeed, has stolen Southampton's traditional dominance in the passenger and cargo trades to the French and Channel Island ports. This is not the first such enterprise of its kind to sound a word of warning to large industrial installations, settled into outdated working ways and placing confidence in their prestige to see them through changing times. Portsmouth's commercial dock labour force was small and versatile; down at the Camber they had been accustomed to the teamwork necessary to operate a small port. This paid off at the new Albert Johnson and Flathouse Quays, where new methods such as containerised cargoes and fast turn-around times were taken up without all the traumas to which larger, older ports were subject.

At the northern end of the Harbour, screened by mature trees and standing on the foreshore a decent way from the roar of traffic along the A27, stands the most venerable of all the military buildings around the Solent. Portchester Castle, built sometime before AD 300, was the most westerly of the Roman coastal defence system called the Saxon Shore, meaning the English shore most at risk from raids across the North Sea by the Germanic peoples. It is well worth a visit, and getting there by dinghy from the parent boat farther down can be a pleasant way of seeing the sights of the Harbour en route. After a tour of the castle walls it is worth going inland to the attractive old village of Portchester itself, with its street lovingly preserved just a few yards from spreading suburbs and thundering traffic. As well as being one of the oldest, Portchester is one of the best preserved of Roman fortifications in the country. The outer walls, enclos-

Portchester

ing an area of about nine acres, are authentically Roman, or Roman style, construction. They are built mainly of flintstones, originally stacked in frames; through the gaps between them the famous Roman mortar was poured and in time became harder than the stone itself. There is a legend that the Apostle St Paul landed near the castle in the first century of the Christian era, an event perpetuated in the name Paulsgrove east of Portchester.

The Normans added to the castle, as did the Plantagenet Kings. During the Dutch wars of the 17th century it held prisoners of war, and was used for that purpose again during the French Revolutionary and Napoleonic Wars. The Frenchmen at Portchester helped to create the lucrative trade in beautifully made toys, trinkets and ship models, all made from the bones of their meat rations. These were bought by visitors on excursions to see the Frenchies, who sold them for pocket money. Today the best examples, especially of the ship models, might change hands for up to five figures. Less popular with the authorities was another talent of the prisoners for making money – literally. Their counterfeit coins threatened to create commercial havoc when they started to circulate round the Portsmouth area.

If time, tide and weather serve, a visit to Fareham can also make a pleasant dinghy excursion. Fareham Creek, which diverges from the Portchester channel at Hardway, a jolly waterside community now a

Fareham Quay

suburb of Gosport, is pleasant and surprisingly undeveloped along part of its shores. Approaching Fareham by water can still be quite delightful this way. Sadly, the town itself fails to maintain the pleasure. Of all the towns around the Solent, this once attractive inland seaport, still graced by fine Georgian buildings, has been most brutalised by road building. The old waterside area has been gutted to make way for roundabouts, overpasses and dual carriageways for commuter links, caused by Fareham's misfortune to be sited at the crossroads of routes from Portsmouth to Gosport, the main road west to Southampton, and the main Meon Valley road which is a principal link with London and the Midlands. But, if you can survive the traffic in one piece, the town's shops are good and varied. There is a new shopping precinct, not everybody's ideal but it has at least kept trade in the town in the face of the new craze for out-of-town hypermarkets, which have forced up the For Sale hoardings over so many old-established retail businesses. Fareham Sailing and Motor Boat Club occupies a nook on the old waterside, and is a friendly and hospitable place. This might be said of all the small clubs sited around Portsmouth Harbour, and Langstone Harbour to the east. The secret, I think, is that their memberships are drawn more from local people than in the more imposing establishments to which people travel from perhaps miles away to go sailing. Small-boat seamanship is like living and breathing to these South Hampshire people and they appreciate it more than signs of a bulging wallet.

In 1893 Frank Cowper, a devoted cruising man who had the excellent idea of writing a series of pilot books expressly for the rising new generation of small-boat cruisers of his day, made an interesting prediction about Portsmouth Harbour. The Royal Navy then, as for many years after, looked on the whole place as its own, including quite a lot of the shoreline. All the possible deep water was used for warship moorings as far north as Fareham Lake, and elsewhere there were torpedo and gunnery ranges, training establishments (HMS *Excellent*, the gunnery school on Whale Island being the most impressive) and, along quieter shores at the north and west side, magazines. Strangers were eyed suspiciously.

'Yachts are not wanted,' wrote Cowper, 'nor idle people pleasure-seeking. I'm glad I did most of my cruising here from 1872 to 1892. Matters were easier then, before we thought of having to fight with any three other navies. However, there's no knowing what we may come to if certain politicians have their way. Cruising in small yachts in Portsmouth Harbour may resume its former happy-go-lucky tranquillity and the mudlarks may be even thicker than of yore.'

Strangely modern all that sounds. In fact it has happened. The Royal Navy today has no ambitions to take on the rest of the world singlehanded. No more warships are built in the Dockyard, and today's compact Fleet really doesn't take up much room. But what Frank Cowper, a man who very much enjoyed quiet anchorages and peaceful waterways, failed to foresee was a population of yachts and small boats within the Harbour in such numbers as today. He could hardly have complained; though like so many writers who extol their favourite places and pleasures, he may have been quite put out to discover people had taken him at his word and wanted to share these delights. He it was who complained mildly about the crowds of boats – this was at the turn of the century, mark you – on the Hamble River.

At the turn of the century Gosport was the home of two firms world-famous for their services to sailing, the building yard of Camper & Nicholsons, just north of the Portsmouth ferry terminal, and its near neighbour the sail loft of Ratsey & Lapthorn. Gosport has other firms who have made the town's contribution to boating a remarkable one. Blake's, the paint and varnish makers, and more recently Crewsaver, whose range of safety gear, including lifejackets and buoyancy bags for dinghies, is known worldwide. Camper & Nicholsons still has pride of place on the Gosport side; the building sheds are there still, but the work inside consists mainly of fitting-out and maintenance. The company's magnificent cruising yachts are based on fibreglass hulls moulded elsewhere, but it serves a wider circle of yachtsmen than ever with its marina, just north of which lies the Gosport Borough yacht harbour.

Curving out from the shore to the north is the long fuel jetty used by the Royal Fleet Auxiliary refuelling tankers which replenish warships at sea with fuel, spares and stores of all kinds. On the southern side of the ferry terminal is Haslar Lake, at the mouth of which submarines lie at the berths at HMS *Dolphin*. The creek runs well inland and can be explored by dinghy upstream to where it changes its name to Alverstoke Lake. At the seaward end, just beyond the submarine berths, is the Joint Services Sailing Centre, the home of not only yachts owned by Service units for the use of their personnel, but also privately-owned yachts belonging to past and serving owners. Upstream of this a new road bridge makes a useful short-cut between Gosport town and Haslar, or as the Services yacht base is known, HMS *Hornet*, after yet another shore establishment. Before this was built a few years back, the creek was crossed by a high and rickety narrow structure which because of its exposure to the breeze earned the nickname Pneumonia Bridge.

A glance at the chart showing the three adjacent harbours of Portsmouth, Langstone and Chichester shows that a 'back door' channel linking all three would be a great convenience for small craft. In fact it is there, but low road and rail bridges and the lack of water at most states of the tide make it less attractive than first thought. In the late 1960s, for the first time since the Second World War, Portsea Island became a true island surrounded by navigable water and could be circumnavigated in a small enough boat.

11   Langstone and Chichester

PORTSMOUTH Harbour shows the city's workaday frontage, the Dockyard and the commercial quays. On the east side Langstone Harbour is more the city's leisure lake. Only a generation or so ago the waters at its northern end were as lonely as anywhere around the Solent, the haunts of wildfowl and solitude-seeking yachtsmen, where the only man-made sound was that of a passing train on the Portsmouth–Havant line. Development has gone apace, but Langstone, now well stocked with yachts like every other Solent harbour, is still a pleasant place for an inland sail. It virtually empties at low water, so the tides rule any exploratory visit. Except for the low factory buildings and flats on the Portsea Island side, the land around Langstone still looks countrified despite the growth of Havant and Bedhampton, particularly the Hayling Island shore on the east side which is generously wooded. The traffic on Portsmouth's fast Eastern Road running north along the shore provides a non-stop background hum. Portsmouth, Langstone and Chichester share several characteristics of landscape. Their common feature of most urgent interest to small-boat navigators is the speed of the tidal streams that flow in and out of the very narrow entrances. Portsmouth's is the most sheltered of the three. Langstone is more exposed to a breeze with any south in it, raising a steep sea on the ebb, aggravated by the seas stumbling and breaking on the broad East and West Winner Sands which have been a fatal trap for many craft in bad weather. But in good weather, timed to carry the flood through the entrance, the approach is easy enough if it is begun well out, to avoid cutting the corners of the Winners. From Langstone Fairway buoy leading marks line up to guide a helmsman in. Langstone, like so many Solent harbours, has its hook-shaped bank of shingle on the west side of the entrance that curves round inside to create Eastney Lake, where a motley collection of craft line the shore (some very permanently) in contrast to the brand new Langstone Marina.

On the northwestern edge of Eastney Lake are the remains of the old lock gates of the canal that once ran inland to the centre of Portsmouth,

Langstone Harbour

part of a larger system which once linked the Thames with the South Coast. It was planned in the early 1800s as a ship canal, but like most canal schemes the grand plans shrank to a much more humble reality. Narrow barges could reach Portsmouth by way of the Thames, the Wey and the Arun, however. From a point just north of Littlehampton a connecting link was dug to Chichester, where there are still quays around a basin close to the city centre. From Chichester, the final stage to Portsmouth used the main Chichester Harbour channels to Emsworth and entered Langstone by the northern end of Hayling Island, thence to those locks on the Portsea Island shore at Milton. One of Langstone's several sailing clubs is sited nearby, called Locks SC.

Clear of the busy southern end, and despite the nearness of Portsmouth and the busy road and railway along its northern shore, Langstone becomes a surprisingly peaceful cruising ground with enough water on the tide to reach the little wilderness of Farlington Marshes and the cluster of islands, little more than reedy mudbanks, which help to screen the drabness of Portsmouth. But in fairness to that city, most of the buildings on the east side stand well back from the water, leaving green open spaces. Portsmouth's schools sailing centre is located here and, about half a mile to the north, close to the muddy creek which makes Portsea a real island when the tide's in, is Tudor Sailing Club, one of Portsmouth's youngest but with a numerous fleet of small cruisers.

Far away on the other side of the harbour, and a much better proposition than the ditch between Portsea and the mainland, the channel from Langstone into Chichester Harbour can easily be followed by small sailing boats, provided they can lower their masts if necessary to pass under the road bridge onto Hayling from Havant. Just to the left of this is the old railway bridge which has a narrow gap cut in its span to allow masted craft through. Timing the tides on this passage is very important as the water virtually drains away on the ebb, leaving a stranded crew with several hours on the soft mud in which to practise the philosophical virtues of patience.

Chichester Harbour, with its long winding channels skirting well-wooded shores and leading to tiny, delightful old ports like Bosham, Dell Quay, Itchenor and Thorney, is a paradise for centreboard craft, which can wander (with care) from the deep-channel markers at high tide. Sadly, it shares the fate of most Solent waterways in becoming packed with craft in the season; its miles of sheltered water has made it one of the most concentrated small boat centres in the South. Even so, it is a lovely place to explore at leisure, in a boat the smaller the better. If you plan to stay in the harbour for a spell, either at half-tide anchor or on a visitor's mooring, it is important to consult the Harbourmaster's pontoon at Itchenor to check on permitted places. Visiting boats, even the smallest, may qualify for dues.

For dinghies and dayboats, a voyage into Chichester could well start from the Langstone Harbour side, by way of the Langstone Channel. Dinghies need masts that are easily unstepped for the passage under the road bridge to Hayling Island from Havant. The clearance here is only about 7 feet at high water and the tide can be strong, so a good plan is to stop before reaching the bridges (the other one is the old Hayling railway bridge), lower the mast and mount the outboard or row. This sounds like trouble, but in a very small boat it will save the uncertainties of the outside passage in anything of a breeze. Chichester's entrance is the most exposed of the three sister harbours, all right when good weather can be relied on but a bit daunting at other times. In a southerly breeze, when big seas from the open Channel are breaking white on the Pole Sands, it is a good place to avoid.

Just inside Sandy Point the channel forks to the right to run for five or six miles towards Chichester. A centreboarder might make it as far as Dell Quay if a visit to the cathedral city of Chichester is planned. In a deeper draft boat, the best plan would be to check first on an available berth in Chichester Yacht Basin (the lock gates stand open an hour or more each side of high water) and pick up a bus to Chichester on the main road a short walk inland.

In contrast to Portsmouth Harbour, Langstone and Chichester were remote places until the years between the wars. In Chichester particularly, there is still much of this remoteness to be discovered, when the bend in a channel screens the rest of the world behind well-wooded countryside. For a boat that can sit on the mud at low tide, there is even a chance of finding a quiet corner of some creek to which the moorings have not yet extended.

Chichester Harbour entrance

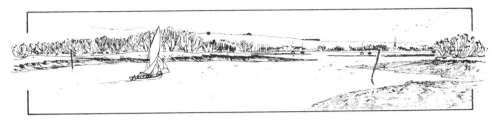

Looking towards Dell Quay

Bosham (locals pronounce it Bozzam) is on everybody's itinerary on a visit to Chichester and gets a bit crowded. It was here, and not at Southampton, that King Canute is supposed to have played the fool with the tide by commanding it to retreat from the royal toes. But in fairness to Canute, one should remember that this little demonstration, if it happened, was designed to censure the flattery of his sycophantic courtiers rather than from any belief that the tide would do as it was told. Bosham is on the Bayeux Tapestry as the place from which King Harold sailed on his fateful journey to Normandy, where his ill-advised promise to Duke William over the succession of the English crown led to the troubles of 1066 and all that. A few centuries earlier Viking raiders are said to have

Emsworth

tried to sail off with the bells of Bosham Church, but their weight swamped the boat. So the bells still may lie somewhere in the mud, and in the best of local traditions they ring in ghostly echo from down below whenever the present church bells are rung.

Emsworth, on the Hampshire–Sussex border, is a good place to replenish supplies. The shops are excellent (including a first class bookshop) and it is well placed for expeditions into the countryside or to the small villages on the slopes of the Downs to the north. With a small cruising dinghy, with a canvas cover to sling over the boom at night, Chichester and Langstone can offer a whole holiday of peaceful cruising, with just enough navigational problems to solve to keep one's seamanship skills bright and sharp.

Birdham Pool

12 Shoals

PEOPLE who don't sail, and who are unfamiliar with the Solent and the lie of the land underwater, are often puzzled by the elaborate hairpin track taken by big ships as they enter or leave Southampton Water. To the innocent eye watching from Cowes Front, the tanker or liner that turns sharp west after leaving Calshot seems obviously bound for Hurst and the Needles Channel. But after a mile or so she makes another tight turn and is heading east, passing through Cowes Roads on her way after all towards the Nab. On the surface, Southampton Water seems to open wide to welcome big vessels: in fact, it can be quite coy. However well buoyed the channel may be between Calshot Spit and the large mid-Solent Brambles shoal, faultless pilotage is required to bring a large tanker, container ship or liner through this chicane. Several, famous liners among them, have touched and stuck embarrassingly fast. No wonder that captains and pilots get very annoyed when yachts stray across their confined track in that couple of miles.

Visiting yacht skippers have several times chanced their luck and sought to gain a few yards in a race, by standing too close to a big ship's bows. None has been known to try it twice, because in addition to the Southampton Harbour byelaw which expressly gives large vessels right of way over yachts in the deep channels, the yacht clubs which organise Solent racing have long made this an underlined warning on their course cards. An offending skipper can be not only disqualified from the race in which he is sailing but runs the risk of a fine if the passage of a big ship is impeded.

The Brambles Bank is a giant wedge of shingle and mud, its base along the shore between Warsash and Lee-on-Solent and its apex due north of

Cowes. Its western end is shallowest, indeed quite large coasters and ferries leave Southampton via the North Channel on the eastern side of the mid-Solent hump. The Brambles might be beneficial to Southampton in one way. Perfectly sheltered against westerly and southwesterly weather, Southampton Water is wide open to winds from the southeast, which can bring a large swell rolling into the East Solent from the open Channel. Lay a ruler on the chart on a line from the Nab to Calshot to see how this could roll on up Southampton Water, were it not damped by the shoals extending from the eastern shore. The Brambles is probably built by the fast ebb stream leaving Southampton Water and trending west to merge with the main stream in the Solent, whereas the tidal stream is comparatively weak on the east side and lacks the power to scour a channel. At its western end there is a knoll, marked by a post painted Dayglow orange, and it is around here, during the exceptional fall of tide that comes with the equinoxes in March and September, that the Brambles actually shows above the surface. Here hardy souls, Uffa Fox and his mates among them, have landed from dinghies to play a game of cricket. A symbolic game, I suspect: the plateau, when the water recedes for an hour or two, is not exactly the turf at Lord's but potted with puddled craters. These games still go on, and are probably enjoyed at the bar afterwards more than on that dismal spot.

On the north side of the dredged channel leading to Southampton Water lies another, smaller shoal, Calshot Spit, important enough to be marked by a lightfloat where the channel curves round it to the north. There is water inshore of the lightfloat for small craft, but not too far in. A sailing chum of long ago made an art of eyeing yachts beating out of Southampton Water and assessing, when they stood on the inshore tack too long, just when they would grind to a halt and announce their mistake to the world with started sheets. He became uncannily good at it and was usually right to within a few seconds. In those days two or three yachts at a time might have been caught there, trying to catch the last of the tide. Today you seldom see one. Perhaps pilotage is better, or perhaps there is less tacking and more motor.

Westward from Cowes the general rule is that the deeper water, therefore the stronger tides, run closer to the Island shore. Close in on that side the streams are forced up and over a series of rocky ledges which at low tide warn of their presence as dark seaweedy patches just below the surface. Off Gurnard, just to the west of Cowes, is the most extensive of these, a spine of sandy rock about a quarter of a mile offshore from near Egypt Point to Gurnard Head. Beyond that is Thorness Bay, where the land recedes with the false invitation of an anchorage but which is bestrewn with reefs and rocky patches. Westward again is Saltmead Ledge, which lies across the path of small boats working in close to cheat a tide.

As the low cliffs on the Island shore drop to the low-lying entrance to Newtown, a broad shelf of gravel prevents any corner-cutting for a boat approaching from the east. On the other side of Newtown yet another reef extends from Hamstead Point, over which the tide clatters merrily. But Hamstead buoy and a barrier of stakes running out a short way from the shore make this impossible to miss. On shore just about here is a giant wedge of concrete, a ramp built during the Second World War for beach landing practice in advance of D-Day. Back at Thorness, just traceable on the shore, are the rusting remains of a more famous wartime relic: the fuel pipes called PLUTO, laid across the Channel to France to supply the Allied armies. There used to be an optimistic joke that after the war the pipes might be used to send French wines the opposite way. This was never taken up.

The chain of inshore obstacles continues west of Yarmouth with a hazard called Black Rock. Sconce Point thrusts another obstacle out from the land, and there are ledges and reefs in the three bays, Colwell, Totland and Alum (where the coloured sands come from), before the great wall of chalk rears high above the Needles. The whole series might be called the Island's Little Barrier Reef and their location is important to tide-cheating racing yachts or those seeking an inshore anchorage. In a breeze they can set up a lively sea, but that is to be expected.

A far more eerie encounter was on a calm summer night in a small dinghy ghosting westward, trying to make Hurst for a dawn start towards Poole. Carried by the tide, she was going at a merry rate over the ground. Gurnard buoy, black and unlit, announced its presence ahead with a gurgling bow wave which gleamed faintly in the summer near-dark. The buoy motorboated away to port and then, as the silence and tranquillity returned, came the sudden and startling sensation of the boat swerving sideways, as if she had fouled a mooring line. An upwelling from the dark water below had swung her right off course. All in silence, but with a dramatic suggestion of great strength at work somewhere down there in the dark that made the episode a quite spooky experience. But then, our imaginations always work better in the dark.

13 The Nab

JUST before Christmas 1982 the lifeboat from Bembridge on the Isle of Wight made its last journey to the Nab Tower, five miles offshore, bearing its annual cargo of Christmas gifts and cheer to the lighthouse keepers. The tower, like so many other offshore lights around our coasts, was going automatic. But what would have surprised the men who built the old structure more than 60 years before was that it was still going strong, certainly stronger than it looks. Compared with the streamlined efficiency of a purpose-built light tower, the Nab looks like something put together with a giant Meccano set. But it has done its job remarkably well. Nearly all the big ships, whether merchantmen and ferries bound to and from Southampton Water, or warships in and out of Portsmouth, arrive and depart through the wider and safer eastern end of the Solent. They have done for many years, which means that the rusty tower must be a familiar sight to quite a few of the world's mariners. It lacks the attractive appearance and dramatic setting of the Needles lighthouse at the western end, but the tonnage of shipping that has been guided by its flashing light (white when seen from seaward, red from the inshore side) must be vastly greater.

The tower, originally one of a pair, was built at Shoreham late in the First World War for anti-submarine defence. The war ended before they were ready. One was scrapped and the survivor was towed to the Nab Shoal, a vast area of shallow water to seaward of Spithead, and sunk in 60 feet of water at its southeast tip. It was not quite a perfect operation as the tower settled with a slight (2½°) list from vertical, but its massive concrete base was able to cope and the structure took the place of a lightship which had been stationed at the edge of the shoal since 1812. Many skippers have mourned the change, because a lightship lying to her mooring was a useful indicator of the direction of the tidal flow, but there could have been no doubt that this big, unbeautiful tower was far easier to spot when approaching from seaward.

It was never the place to encourage daydreams about being a lighthouse keeper. On top of the enormous cylindrical body, surrounded by a web of steel girders, were some flimsy and vulnerable looking tin huts which hinted at pretty abominable conditions for living and working in bad weather. The noise of the wind shrieking through that mass of steel and galvanised sheeting must have been pretty dreary.

For warships bound in for Portsmouth, the Nab marked virtually the end of the voyage. 'First the Nab, then the Warner, No Man's Fort and Flathouse Corner' went the old lower-deck doggerel although, being lower deck, an unprintable first syllable was substituted in the penultimate word. The Warner was once a lightship, like the Nab. Today it marks the narrow channel between the shoals that reach out from Island on the port hand and from Southsea to starboard. Its wheezing fog whistle is one of the Solent's more distinctive sounds.

Yachts seldom pass close to the Nab. Bound from the south towards Portsmouth or Cowes, they would enter the eastern end of the Solent about 3½ miles west of the tower, using Bembridge Ledge buoy as their mark. Approaching down-Channel from the east, they might be a mile or more north of it in shaping a course from the Owers to the Warner. Off Portsmouth, however, are two structures which nobody can avoid passing close to, unless maybe they are small-boat fishermen who know their way between the remains of the defensive obstructions running to both the Island and mainland shores. Standing like two squat gateposts to Portsmouth and beyond are Horse Sand Fort to starboard and No Man's Land Fort to port. Before these are abeam, the third of the trio, Spit Sand

The Forts guarding the Eastern approach to the Solent

Fort, can be seen, close off Southsea and on the west side of the approach channel into Portsmouth Harbour. Actually there is a fourth, the smaller St Helen's Fort which guards the entrance to Bembridge Harbour. It is probably the best looking of all, though often hard to spot in the shadow of the high land behind.

These three remarkable chunks of masonry, which seem capable of defying the elements to doomsday if they are left to it, were built during another French scare, 350 years after Henry VIII built his chain of defences along the Solent, which are remarkably handsome structures. Not that the simple outlines of Palmerston's Victorian defences are ugly in themselves. What is ugly is the assortment of rusty iron which can be glimpsed on the top of the masonry. King Henry built his forts ashore, at narrow places, because gunnery in Tudor times was a primitive, inaccurate and short-range business. By the 1860s, when a period of Francophobia was causing jitters in the corridors of military power, warships could throw shells too far to be repulsed by forts ashore and had to be stopped farther out. Steam power had rendered blockading obsolete, so for the first time in centuries Britain fell back on defence as a strategy, instead of following the naval tradition of making the enemy's coast her frontier.

The Victorians seem to have feared that an invasion from the French was more likely than it had been from Napoleon 50 years before. Enormous labour and expense were put into constructing these Spithead forts, and a whole chain of shore forts and batteries protecting Portsmouth and Gosport on their landward sides. In time-honoured fashion, a committee was formed to decide the form these should take. As Garry Mitchell reveals in his detailed history of the forts, Army officers, not too well versed in the effects of structures on tides and navigable channels, advocated a fixed barrier across Spithead. But after arguments against this, obviously being the hindrance to navigation and, less obviously, the unforeseen long-term effects of silting, the Commission decided on island forts, as had been suggested a few years before by Colonel W.F.D. Jervois, the Assistant Inspector General of Fortifications. The crucial part played in the American Civil War by Fort Monroe in the fight between the warships *Monitor* and *Merrimac* was fresh in the planners' minds in coming to their decision.

The forts never fired a shot in anger, but by a strange twist, more than 80 years after they were built they trained their guns on a French warship – the very purpose for which they had been designed. In 1940, facing the most serious invasion threat for centuries, the Government decided to immobilise or seize the French Fleet. Several warships were at Portsmouth, including the battleship *Courbet*. To cover their seizure the forts' guns were brought into readiness and trained on the French vessels. Fortunately it was a bloodless takeover, because had she decided to make a run for it *Courbet* could have soon dealt with the sea forts and their old armour. During the First World War they had been brought to readiness but stood idle, the Channel being virtually closed to German surface ships. In the Second War, they might have played a part in protecting Portsmouth against the blitz, but they could not have stood the weight of mounting heavy modern anti-aircraft guns.

After the Army withdrew its garrisons for good in 1956, the forts were put up for sale. Spit Sand was sold in 1982, No Man's Land went to a property company in 1985 for conversion to a luxury home. St Helen's has been sold also, it is understood, but the Ministry of Defence has taken Horse Sand off the market and has retained it.

No Man's Land and Horse Sand Forts are not the islands they appear. Between each one and the shore, at Ryde and Southsea respectively, is a line of concrete blocks and piles laid to obstruct a possible attack by small, fast torpedo boats of shallow draft. These barriers, put there about five years before the First World War, remain today, obliging craft to pass between the forts instead of inshore of them, although there is a gap in the Horse Sand barrier close inshore at Southsea, a useful short-cut for small craft coasting between Chichester and Portsmouth Harbours. This boat passage is marked by beacons.

14   Solent Craft

BEFORE the vehicle ferries took over the cross-Solent freight trade, enabling lorries to travel across instead of transferring their loads to barges at Southampton's Town Quay or Portsmouth's Camber Docks, one of the jolly sights of the Solent, and a change from the yachting scene, was to be seen from Cowes seafront on a breezy day when a fleet of black and grey motor barges, having carried the ebb down the Medina from Newport, set off with the first of the new flood bound across for the mainland. Several survived from sailing days until the end of the trade in the early 1970s. Although engined, they still carried chainplates, leeboard hoisting tackles, even sheet horses. The stumpy mast survived, as did the spar that on a sailing barge would have been the sprit, and the pair made a useful crane. Off the Prince Consort buoy their ways would divide. Those Portsmouth-bound would turn their transoms to the sea for the dead run towards Gilkicker Point. Southampton-bound barges rolled in the lop until clear of West Bramble, then bore away towards Calshot. Aboard a good few of these craft was a thick, tanned trysail which was dragged stiff as a plank from the fo'c'sle in a breeze and set from the mast to steady the roll, as fishing boats do.

Wherever a working boat raises a sail of any sort she steals attention from anything around. Those dark brown scraps of steadying sail, nowhere near big enough to provide motive power, nevertheless conjured a sense of adventure around these homely and overlooked craft on their routine crossings. But sometimes even the thumping diesel down below could not quite ensure that a crossing would be routine. I remember another fleeting glimpse of the adventurous side of the trade when one of the barges of the Vectis Shipping Company's fleet got in trouble in a fresh breeze off the wide shoals that run out from the shore at Hill Head, southeast from the Hamble River entrance. She was travelling light, with lots of leeway. Maybe her engine let her down: anyway she could not claw off, so there was nothing for it but to round up and let go the anchor. There she rode until another barge came in close and got a line aboard. Under sail, this sort of uncertainty about timely – or even safe – arrival was always present, even on the 'sheltered' Solent. But fogs and calms were more a bane than blows, and until steam began to appear not long after the Napoleonic Wars, the most reliable way of getting the mails to the Island in light weather was by rowing boat.

The poet John Keats was impressed by an incident involving his sailing ferry on the return to Southampton from his last visit to the Island in August 1819. He described it in a letter to Fanny Brawne:

'One of the pleasant things I have seen lately was at Cowes. The Regent in his Yatch (I think they spell it) was anchored opposite – a beautiful vessel – and all the yatchs and boats on the coast were passing and repassing it; and circuiting and tacking about in every direction. I never beheld anything so silent, light and graceful. As we passed over to Southampton there was nearly an accident. There came by a boat, well manned, with two naval officers at the stern. Our bowlines took the top of their little mast and snapped it off close by the board. Had the mast been stouter they would have been upset. In so trifling an event I could not help

A Cowes Ketch

admiring our seamen. Neither officer nor man in the whole boat moved a muscle – they scarcely noticed it, even with words.'

Keats' craft was probably a gaff-rigged cutter or ketch, well built and maintained. Gaff rig, and sprit rig for smaller vessels, were favourites for Solent work. In his famous collection of minutely accurate engravings of small craft published in 1829, E. W. Cooke drew a Cowes boat, the type of cargo carrier later known as a Cowes ketch. Pretty vessels these, combining the sturdiness of Thames spritsail barges with the grace of West Country schooners. They drew more water than a barge would have done, and were the Island's vital link with the mainland, carrying commodities like beer and flour, roofing tiles and farm machinery, much the same sort of cargoes as their diesel-powered successors did at the end of their working lives. The ketches were well built, as is demonstrated in their long careers. The *Bee*, for example, built by Hansen at East Cowes in 1801, was still working until 1926. The dainty, tiny *Arrow* was built in 1875 and was working cargoes for Shepard Bros. of Newport between the Medina and the mainland until 1938. After the Second World War some of the private fleets were taken under the wing of the nationalised British Road Services, a continuation of the strong railway interest in the Solent cargo traffic before the war.

The Cowes ketches were originally double-ended. Besides those built by Hanse, White of West Cowes built several and the sharp stern developed into a stumpy counter or transom. They might be found anywhere between Poole and Selsey – Langstone and Chichester Harbours had busy small coaster ports until well into this century – and in Southampton Water, Ashlett at the mouth and Eling and Redbridge at the inshore end were three places into which sailing coasters regularly squeezed. When the vogue for spritsail barges was at its height, several were built on the River Itchen at Northam in Southampton, mainly of steel instead of the wood favoured further east. Their rig was the same as that used on the Thames barges.

Cowes gave its name to another, much smaller, working boat. This was the ever useful Cowes waterman's skiff, about 15 feet long, rigged with a staysail, sprit mainsail and small mizzen set close against the transom stern. These were the cabs of the yachting port, on hand at a hail to bring crew or passengers ashore from yachts or other craft anchored in the Roads, or as ferries across the harbour. In the winter months their owners made a living by seine or line fishing. During the summer and particularly during Cowes Week, they were busy taking trippers for a sail around the anchored vessels or as ship-to-shore ferries. A small boat had to be capable to ply this trade in Cowes Roads in any reasonable open-boat weather. The tradition changed very little, surviving the switch from sail to outboard motor power, until the late 1960s. In Cowes, the good upkeep of boats seems to be an instinct and these little water taxis, although not spick and span to yacht standard, had an encouraging look of wellbeing about them. There was less spit and polish bestowed on the Seagull outboards that pushed many of them, salt-caked and with the brass petrol tanks missing a lot of black paint, but they would purr to the first pull and the boatman would know to a rev how much to give his motor to lie alongside a gleaming hull with hardly a touch. Latterly the diminishing community of Cowes watermen made their base at the Fountain Steps beside the ferry pontoon. Much of their work was taken away when marina development enabled yachtsmen to step directly ashore at a berth, and the widespread use of small inflatables for a quick harbour dash meant the loss of more.

In the Southampton Maritime Museum, overlooking the Town Quay from where the barges once sailed for Cowes and Newport, there is a small model of one of the type, the *Bee*. Also there is a fine model of another Solent passenger-carrying craft which became something of a byword for seaworthiness, and its crews too for venturing where other boatmen durst not. This was the Spithead wherry. The Southampton example is the *Woodham*, made from the lines taken off the original boat in 1936 by W. M. Blake for the Coastal Craft Sub-Committee of the Society for Nautical Research. The Spithead wherries were big; *Woodham*, smaller than some, was 27 feet overall, with a beam of 8 feet and a depth of hull of more than 4 feet with room under the bottom boards for ballast. She was clinker planked and framed with oak. Wherries were big because their work took them on the wide waters between Portsmouth and Ryde, and to ships anchored in St Helen's Roads off the Island's eastern end, waters which were too open for skiffs. In the days of the sailing Navy, wherries, manned by men and sometimes women who must have been as tough as nails as well as superb boat sailors, would be on hand among the ships for a hail for a fare or an errand. Sometimes they were there when the flag signal was made that no boats from the ships were to be hoisted out because of the weather. They were big enough to carry any cargo within reason, even livestock sometimes, and handy enough to go anywhere. They became such an important part of Solent transport that their scale of charges was fixed by law; in July 1822 the Justices at Winchester fixed the rate for passage between Portsmouth and Ryde as five shillings (25 new pence) for a wherry with one man and seven shillings (35 new pence) for two or more men. For the longer crossing between Southampton and Cowes a two-man boat could charge 12 shillings and sixpence, and a four-man boat a guinea. The extra hands on this run hinted that the sweeps might be got out if the breeze fell away.

A remarkable amount of small-boat work was done in the Solent under oars. I read an account somewhere of a boat from the pilot cutter *Diligence*, which used to be anchored in Southampton Water near Hythe before the shore station which took its name was built, putting the pilot aboard an outward bound steamer which took in tow the boat and its crew of a man and a boy, as far as the Needles. There the pilot left the steamer and re-embarked in the boat, which then returned to Southampton under oars. Presumably there was no incoming ship requiring his services with an easy homeward pluck for the rowers.

Wherrying was a family business over several generations. Smaller, or second-class wherries, were used for sheltered water work around Portsea Island and as ferries across Portsmouth Harbour. They were maintained to a high standard, as the Portsmouth boatbuilder George Feltham, who started work in Queen Victoria's reign, well remembered. Like the taxis on land, wherries were inspected by the Watch Committee or its local equivalent, so there was strong incentive to keep boats looking smart. All part of the service was the pieces of oilcloth carried to cover the thwarts in a shower so that they would be dry for future passengers.

In winter or bad weather an open-water passage in a wherry, however well handled, must have been an ordeal. A canvas cuddy might be rigged forward to protect the unhappy passengers from the worst of the spray, but in an open boat water and cold draughts find their way everywhere. The steam ferries when they came must have been hailed with relief.

To cruising yachtsmen of a generation ago, the working boat that came closest to the ideal small, shallow-draft boat, with scope for variations in size and layout, was still the dainty little gaff cutter popularly known as the Itchen Ferry type, although boats like it could be found in practically all the Solent harbours. Itchen Ferry was the small waterside community, the nucleus of what is now Woolston, on the east bank of the River Itchen just before it combines with the estuary of the River Test to form Southampton Water. Since the mid-1970s the name (still used by local people) has been rendered obsolete by the road bridge across the Itchen. Though cut off from Woolston proper by the Southampton–Portsmouth railway line, it maintained its identity until the Second World War when it was virtually obliterated by German bombers seeking the Supermarine aircraft factory which stood on the water's edge close by. Today it has lost out to a motley collection of single-storey factory buildings. Afloat, however, lie two or three surviving Itchen Ferry cutters, still working under sail and with their Southampton fishing numbers with the prefix su painted on their bows.

In its day, Itchen Ferry bred small-boat sailors like the Diapers and the Parkers and others, in demand by the owners of the big racing yachts as skippers and crews. One of them, Ben Parker, the owner of his own fishing boat, was sailing master of the Kaiser's yawl *Meteor II*. In 1902 he went to America to sail home the big schooner, another *Meteor*, built there for the German emperor. Tom Diaper was another of Itchen Ferry's famous yacht masters and in 1890 he sailed the 77 ton cutter *Valkyrie* for Lord Dunraven.

This was summer work. While they were away winning prestige for their yachts' owners, their small fishing cutters were laid up to be fitted out for the winter's work ahead. Boats of the type were used from the Hamble River for shellfish and until the early years of this century there was friendly rivalry between the two waterside communities. There was keen racing of these working boats at regatta days, when flags fluttered and bands played, and the racing – competing boats then had to lie at anchor with sails lowered until the starting gun – was of the standard that made Southampton Water men the darlings of wealthy yacht skippers. These close links with what was new in yachting was reflected in the smartness of the cutters, and the care that went into their design by men like Payne and, the most famous, Dan Hatcher upriver at Northam. The boats were built of the cheapest good materials, but red pine planking could stand the pace as well as more exotic yacht woods like mahogany and teak, as several of these remarkably long-lived craft have shown. The most famous of Hatcher's cutters, the 21 foot *Nellie*, carefully cherished by later owners, still drew admiring gazes on the Solent until recently. She made an interesting comparison with another Hatcher boat, the *Wonder*, also blessed with careful ownership into a good-looking old age. *Nellie* was built in 1866 and *Wonder* in 1860. Smaller still, and older, was the little *Flutt* which after 40 or more years of work was fitted with a centreboard, later removed and an outside ballast keel hung underneath.

Even the smallest of Southampton's craft had a distinctive grace. Not long ago a cluster of them used to have moorings tucked in the small space of water between the Town Quay and the Royal Pier. Their topsides were painted black with a cove line in white. Inside, the standard finish was buff. Rowing versions tended to be carvel built, rather fine at the bow and with low freeboard. Those fitted with sailing gear were, of course, fuller. J. W. Holness of Woolston drew the lines of survivors of the type for an article in the *Yachting Monthly Annual* of 1972, which remains the best concise survey of Southampton's small working boats. *Bream*, one of the last surviving of these sail-and-oar 14-footers, has been restored to exhibition standard. She was built in 1910 by G. Cozens, an employee in the Paynes yard; he charged £19 for her. She is now on show in the Southampton Maritime Museum which when it soon moves to larger premises may be able to house an Itchen Ferry cutter.

Holness writes: 'A friend, whose father used to fish out of the Itchen, recalls being kept off school in the afternoons when about ten or eleven to help his father row their 13 foot rowboat down Southampton Water into the Solent, a distance of about eight miles, to set drift nets for herring which arrived in the Solent in the Autumn. During October they would leave Itchen at about one o'clock, arriving at the ground in time to shoot the net at dusk, the 'dark shoot'. If there were any fish in the net when they hauled they shot again and, after hauling, set off back with the flood tide, arriving back at about seven or eight o'clock. If the wind was fair they set a small lugsail. If not, they rowed. If no fish resulted from the 'dark shoot' they came straight back, for to shoot again was a waste of time. Late in the autumn the herring would come up to Netley [about two miles south of Itchen, on the east side of Southampton Water], so that he and his father would get there at dusk if he rushed straight down from school to the boat. Usually the catches were collected by various fish merchants, but it was not unknown for a fisherman's wife to take it to Southampton by boat if they lived in a village nearby.

'As indicated by the name, the rowboats were propelled mainly by oars, especially the smaller ones. Sometimes they were referred to as "the 14-footers" when about that length, or simply as "the little boat" when the owner also owned a smack. The smallest ones were about 12–13 feet long and were commonest on the Itchen. Many did not carry any sailing gear at all.'

Common rig originally for the 14-footers was a sprit (locally 'spleet') mainsail and foresail, but by the turn of the century this was replaced by the standing lug main, cut very high-peaked so that the yard only needed a jaws at its foot to turn it into a gunter lug, as on *Bream*. According to Holness, it gave a better performance than the spritsail, but the advantage of the spritsail was that it could be easily bundled up out of the way when the crew needed room for fishing. An interesting feature of *Bream*, possibly reflecting the Itchen men's being more receptive to new yachting ideas, is that she has a centreboard, which became popular on Southampton Water about the time the standing lug rig was adopted.

Hard as was their life in those days of sail and oar, watermen seemed to have spent a remarkable amount of time afloat just for fun. Upstream at Northam, a club was formed in the 1870s that raced 13 foot rowboats, called punts by Dixon Kemp, which may have had an influence on the form of their working counterparts. These boats, deep and heavy by today's standards, were used by yacht skippers and shipyard foremen for recreation.

Itchen-built boats lasted well, it was claimed because local builders traditionally believed in thoroughly impregnating all the wood in them with linseed oil before painting. This old trick is being rediscovered in the current revival of interest in restoring old craft.

Steam arrived on the Solent in 1815, nine days before the Battle of Waterloo. Or rather, the first steam vessel seen on the Solent passed through, on her delivery voyage from the Clyde to London. She was the 49 ton steam yacht *Thames*, under the command of a Captain Dodd. The 76 foot wooden hulled paddler made an impressive passage down the Irish Sea and round Cornwall before putting into Portsmouth. On this, the first open-sea voyage undertaken by a British steam vessel, she caused a stir by heaving-to and passing some mail across to the Waterford packet, and off the Cornish coast she stopped to rescue the occupants of a swamped excursion boat. Many thoughtful people who saw her smoky passage up the Solent from the Needles must have realised that the days of dreary crossings to the Island by sail and oar, which could take anything from a spray-soaked 2½ hours in a breeze or up to seven hours in light airs, were numbered. Just three years later George Ward of Northwood, near Cowes, set up the first regular service between Southampton and Cowes with the *Prince of Coburg*. The Press enthused. The *Hampshire Telegraph* reported that the vessel began her service at the end of July 1820, just a year after John Keats's ferry had tangled with the naval barge, 'as a regular Post Office packet. She performed the voyage to Cowes and back three times in a day . . . part of which was necessarily against wind and tide. This fine vessel must be a great convenience to passengers, particularly in calms when only open boats may be used. Her velocity in a calm sea, even against the tide, is about 8 knots.'

With such convenience, speed and comfort available (passengers could actually sit in a cabin, in the warm and dry) it was not long before other services were in operation. But it was a few years before the terminals matched the convenience of the ferries themselves. Fountain Quay at Cowes was not modified until 1824, and in Southampton, when the Royal Pier was opened in 1833 it marked the end of passengers having to be taken to and from the ferry by boats. At Ryde there had been added hardship, in addition to the discomfort of the crossing under sail or oars. The author of a guidebook on Ryde, published about the middle of the 19th century, recalled: 'It was customary except during the short interval of High Water for the passengers to be crammed into a common luggage cart and then drawn over the sands and through the waves till it reached a depth sufficient for a boat to float alongside it, into which they were transferred and conveyed off to the packet . . . This could not have been inviting at the best of times, but was really terrific to weak and timid persons during the concurrence of a fresh gale, driving rain and the tide, perhaps at its lowest ebb, to say nothing of the horrors of landing in a dark and squally night.' Ryde's first pier, which eased this misery, built in 1814 and rebuilt in 1818 after storm damage, was extended in 1824 and 1833 and finally replaced by the present long structure in 1880. The generous endowment of railway from the pierhead station to the Island hinterland was the result of the Southern Railway taking over the pier in 1924.

Down west, at Yarmouth, the perils and discomforts of crossings to Lymington by sail and oar must have been even worse, with the stronger tides of the West Solent stirring up a dangerous sea in any breeze. But travel by road was so bad that passengers from the west used to brave it rather than face the extra land journey, if they were able to catch a packet to a destination at the eastern end. So there was great joy in Yarmouth in 1829 when it was announced that a steamer, the *Duke of Buccleugh*, would operate a triangular service linking Lymington, Yarmouth and Portsmouth. But she was switched to the more lucrative Cowes–Southampton run, and Yarmouth had to wait another year before the 52 foot *Glasgow* started the service; she also ran to Cowes, Southampton and Ryde on certain days. *Glasgow* pioneered a Solent ferry practice which survived until the 1930s: she towed a lighter to carry horses, cattle and private carriages.

Human nature being what it is, the novelty of being able to cross in comfort and to time began to wear off, and the memories of those pre-steam journeys began to fade. The steamers, like the railways at the same time, had to bear with complaints ranging from overcharging in the saloon buffet to having to share the decks with livestock. In 1866 a wooden paddler, the *Vectis*, was the first vessel built for the company conveniently known to this day as Red Funnel Steamers but whose full name reads like a litany: The Southampton, Isle of Wight and South of England Royal Mail Steam Packet Company. (With new business titling trends, they now could add two words, so that it reads Public Limited Company.) Red Funnel Steamers have moved with the times. They introduced hydrofoils for fast passenger services to Cowes, and a large part of their fleet are the tugs which share the movement of ships at Southampton Docks and the Esso Fawley marine terminal with vessels of the Alexandra Towing Company, which hails from Liverpool. Red Funnel vessels have had remarkably long careers. The 122 ton *Vectis*, which carried a jolly figurehead – 'a likeness of the young lady who launched her [Miss Elizabeth Lamb, the daughter of the company chairman] represented as wearing a turban hat and a white yachting jacket trimmed with gold' – was not withdrawn from service until 1910. Another more recent old-timer was the *Lord Elgin*, bought into the Red Funnel fleet in 1909 and later converted to a cargo vessel with a large derrick crane mounted on deck. She remained in the fleet until 1955 when she was replaced with a war surplus tank landing craft renamed *Norris Castle* for the growing vehicle traffic to Cowes.

From the mid-19th century until the outbreak of the Second World War and a few years after, steamer excursions on the Solent, in addtion to the regular scheduled ferry crossings, were immensely popular and attracted more than a dozen companies to share the profitable trade. And these were not confined to Solent waters. The big paddle steamers of the late 19th and early 20th century days were remarkable seaboats. There were excursions round the Island, across Poole Bay to Bournemouth or Weymouth, or even, for braver souls and in good weather, cross-Channel ventures to Cherbourg and the Channel Islands. Today ferries on the main Solent routes are divided into two types: the fast vessels like the Southampton–Cowes hydrofoils and the new catamaran type craft on the Portsmouth–Ryde route, introduced by Seaspeed; or the slower passenger car services, also from Southampton and Portsmouth. The latter's Island terminal is at Fishbourne at the mouth of Wootton Creek. On these, and between Lymington and Yarmouth, for a sea voyage rather than a tame but fast commuter crossing, the vehicle service is recommended. One can go as a foot passenger, and there are buffets and saloons in which to sit and look at the passing parade of yachts and large vessels; or if the weather is fine, pace the deck and lean over the rail, without which a Solent crossing loses much of its fun for holidaymakers.

The oldest ferry still in regular operation plies a shorter route, across the Hamble River from the village of Hamble on the west bank to Warsash on the east side. The first record of a ferry dates from the end of the 15th century. The Tudor traveller John Leland crossed the Hamble here in the 1530s, and until well after the Second World War the crossing was maintained by rowing boats with Jack Bevis in charge. But with the building of a new road bridge upstream at Bursledon in the 1930s, to replace the old wooden toll bridge that slowed down the traffic, the ferry suffered a steady decline, although local people still prefer the quick water crossing rather than the six or seven-mile detour by road.

Jack Bevis continued to be the ferryman until he was 80 years old, but then took an assitant, Ray Sedgwick. In February 1958, when Bevis retired, he took over as ferryman. He has a clinker launch with an inboard diesel engine and can land his passengers dryshod at the Hamble side on a pontoon. During the great freeze of 1962–3 the launch kept going, dodging floating sheets of ice on the river. Ray Sedgwick is a rare spirit in a restless world where the idea of working unsociable hours is regarded with horror. After an apprenticeship as a toolmaker, he chose the life of getting up before six every morning and linking the two waterside village communities in all weathers, except on Christmas and Boxing Days, and thereby doing his bit to maintain a sense of community among the people of Hamble and Warsash. In Hamble, Petters, the diesel engine makers, struck up an arrangement which did good for them and the ferry service. They used Ray Sedgwick's boats, which had long working days, as testbeds for their engines on which they could see how they stood up to actual working conditions.

Another passenger ferry which like Ray's will carry passengers' bikes when required, is that from Eastney at the southeast corner of Portsea Island to Hayling Island, across the narrow entrance of Langstone Harbour. This short crossing saves a weary road journey all the way round via Havant and is operated by Portsmouth Council.

15 Smuggling

QUICK and easy transport is now so taken for granted that it is hard to realise how isolated were the small waterside hamlets and villages around the Solent until well into this century. The west bank of Southampton had no proper road link between Fawley and Southampton until 1924. Ashlett Creek (now a yacht harbour, overlooked discreetly by Fawley Refinery), the gravel hard at Hythe and the tiny harbour at Eling were still regular ports of call for coasting vessels. Tanned sail spritsail barges and small schooners were the main commercial carriers, handling coal, building materials and grain. People still alive can remember the great adventure of a charabanc excursion, on solid tyres over the uncertain roads from Southampton into the New Forest, or even as far as Bournemouth. If the countryside was as remote to townsfolk until that recently, it was vastly more so two centuries earlier; a factor which, together with the Solent shores' suitability for beach-boat work, made the area the smuggling capital of England.

Geoffrey Morley, in his history of the smuggling trade along the Hampshire and Dorset coasts, described how in the 18th century smugglers virtually ruled the roost in Lymington as an open brotherhood. 'So active were the Lymington smugglers in their heyday that one of the town's leading ladies, the future bride of the poet Robert Southey, complained bitterly that she was awoken practically every night by noisy smugglers passing under her windows. They cared for nobody, not even the Dragoons stationed in the town, who, no doubt, were well bribed anyway . . . By the 1820s the smugglers had such a hold on Lymington that the town's magistrates were said to have sworn in the most notorious of them as Special Constables in order to ensure that some sort of order was kept among their own kind.'

Lymington had a network of underground passages, traces of which still survive, particularly the one linking the Londesborough Hotel (The Nag's Head in smuggling days) and the Angel Inn on the other side of High Street. Another ran from the Angel down the hill to the waterside. The business thrived too along the shore eastward from Lymington to the mouth of Southampton Water. Just offshore of the saltmarshes near Pylewell Lake, east of Lymington River, there is a deep still known as Brandy Hole, a likely place for sinking kegs of contraband until the coast was clear for a landing. Much of the landing from luggers newly arrived from France took place along the southern shores of the Wight; it was then brought overland to the Solent shore and transferred to small boats for the easy crossing to the mainland. Beaulieu River, tree-sheltered and winding, was very popular with smugglers who liked privacy. Tales of melodramatic deterrents against curious strangers are legion: the stuff of jolly smugglers' tales ever since, although in reality the Free Traders were very nasty to those who crossed their path or betrayed them to the Dragoons or the Preventives. Tales of gangland punishment killings in our own time seem vicious and sordid compared with the jolly smuggler image which we today still foster, but smugglers were quite capable of imposing Mafia-like discipline and murdering those who got in their way. The adventure-story image is understandably persistent when tales survive of smugglers uttering frightful howls and moans among the stone walls of Palace House at Beaulieu, formerly the great Abbey, wailing a parody of monkish plainsong to add colour to their scare stories of ghosts.

While the trade all along this shore was thriving, it concerned a small patch of what today looks unpromising shoreline, that Geoffrey Morley cites as 'possibly one of the busiest for smugglers in the whole of the British Isles.' This is Stanswood Bay, which lies between the Beaulieu River entrance and Calshot Spit at the mouth of Southampton Water. A small stream, the Blackwater, runs into the Solent halfway along this gently curving bay. Today it is a mere trickle but at one time it opened out in a small estuary which made a useful harbour for small craft until silting made it unusable in the early 18th century. Inland were woods, scattered farms and cottages and plenty of hiding places. Smuggling here was such a communal industry that Sprat's Down, a hamlet about a mile inland, still has the tag Lazy Town, a relic of smuggling days when local people were busy all night and caught up on their sleep during the daytime. This odd lack of activity during daylight hours was evidently a sure sign of a smuggling stronghold. One visitor to Niton, at the southern tip of the Isle of Wight, wryly noticed a similar sleepiness during a visit there.

Along this Stanswood shore are two spectacular monuments to the openness and efficiency with which the better class of smuggler went about his business. A house called Eaglehurst is one. The other, more familiar because it is conspicuous from the sea, is a red brick structure something like a factory chimney from a distance, standing 110 feet high on top of a low gravelly cliff called Eagle's Cliff. It looks like a folly, but it was anything but when it was designed and built by Temple Simon Luttrell sometime after 1730 as nothing less than a lookout, command post and signal station for his smuggling activities. A better class of smuggler Luttrell certainly was, because he supplied a better class of goods. Only the best brandy, for example, was good enough when you had customers who included members of the Royal Family and sprigs of society. Luttrell's concern for quality led to his undoing: he died in a French prison in 1803, the result, it is said, of being caught on one of his trips across the Channel to test the goods before they were shipped. But it is nice to think that a man of Luttrell's style, and with a romantic spirit inherited from Irish ancestry, might have been siezed by Napoleon's agents not as a mere smuggler – after all, the French approved of this method of undermining the English economy – but as a secret agent, a real-life Scarlet Pimpernel perhaps. We may never know, which in itself is a successful ingredient of romance.

One has to admire a man who could raise the illegal trade to such a pitch of efficiency as to use his tower for displaying signal code flags to vessels waiting in the offing for a safe landing. From the shore below the tower, the goods were taken a short way inland to a warren of caves around Sprats Common just behind Eaglehurst. The rest of a delivery, to Southampton or beyond, was comparatively easy, when concealed under a load of timber, farm produce or whatever on an innocent country wagon. Today Luttrell's Tower, one of the most unusual buildings along the Solent shores, is a handsome piece of property. Its three-storey battlemented base, pierced with elegant Georgian windows with a bow frontage on its eastern side, is topped by the chimney-like lookout tower which rises as high again. A better place to see all the comings and goings along the shore or in the offing could hardly be devised.

It was across the water at Cowes that the Customs Board established a base to combat the Solent smuggling bonanza, and in September 1772 William Arnold took up the job of Collector of Customs. By 1786 Arnold's measures were having an effect in deterring the larger vessels used for cross-Channel runs. Small ones, as always, could slip through the net. Fishermen at the back of the Wight were quite prepared to take a rowing boat across from any one of the small coves near St Catherine's Point to the Cherbourg Peninsula, take on a small, high-value cargo (lace and perfume were in demand, as well as the more bulky brandy) and row home again. Their classic manoeuvre for avoiding capture by a Revenue cutter was to row directly into the wind, forcing the sailing vessel to tack. As a rowing boat's straightline course was shorter than a sailing vessel's zig-zag to windward, the rowers usually got away with it. As these fishermen used their working boats, small enough to be beached and dragged clear of the surf after use, it follows that many such cross-Channel passages were made in open boats little more than 14 feet long, about the same length, though heavier and less handy, as the average sailing dinghy today.

The lore of smuggling, depicting it as a romantic, adventurous activity, is not just nostalgia. The trade employed an army of people ashore, whose job was to run the stuff from hiding places to destinations. Many of these must have been men of spirit who welcomed a break from the lifelong bondage of work on the land. Smugglers were popular men in their own day. To the rich they were useful sources of supply of life's little luxuries. To the poor they were folk-heroes, whose courage and initiative showed many country people a way out of a poor and unpleasant existence.

William Cobbett, with his practised eye for social injustice, told of a countryman who was supposed to feed a family on two shillings and sixpence a week – virtually impossible unless he poached for the pot, which laid him open to shooting by keepers, maiming by mantraps or being beaten up as an example to others. No wonder men took to smuggling to escape the vicious poverty. The heyday of it all was between 1750 and 1840, the result of stiff duties imposed on luxury goods and the growing taste for them. The great days ended with the Corn Law Acts, by which several hundred items carrying duty were removed from the Statute Book. By then, and belatedly, the Coastguard had been formed into a more efficient force to curb the trade.

16 Explore

THERE is water deep enough in the main channels of the Solent to accommodate any vessel afloat. Supertankers bound for the Esso Refinery at Fawley have in the past found the bottom clearance a bit slender for their immense draft, but the practice has been for them to discharge some of their load at the Milford Haven terminal in Wales or off Torquay before heading east to the Solent. As for yachts, the great Victorian and Edwardian cutters and schooners were never too constrained, and even less are the maxis and pre-war deep-keelers that occasionally bring a touch of old-time splendour to the scene today.

But to explore the Solent shores instead of merely to sail its beaten tracks, a small boat, a centreboarder for preference or a twin-keeler which can take the ground upright, multiplies the fun immeasurably. Alternatively, have a proper small dinghy as a tender which can be used for upstream explorations away from the parent craft. Inflatables, useful as they are for short ship-to-shore errands and for stowing partly deflated on deck, don't offer the comforts for a longer voyage and are hard to row.

With most of the Solent estuary harbours packed with moorings in their lower reaches, a boat suitable for seeing the sights upstream is of great value; e.g. beyond the swing bridge at Yarmouth, or upstream of the road and rail bridges on the Hamble, or beyond Buckler's Hard where the deep channel begins to peter out. All offer delights to those who enjoy getting away from the crowd. A small dinghy with a sail or a decent pair of oars (so much of the peace is lost if you can't go anywhere without an outboard buzzing at the back) is the perfect vehicle. Such alternatives to the all too common progress from one marina to another, which is the easy option of small-boat cruising, not only yield more insight into the real Solent hinterland but they also add a sense of achievement to a holiday visit.

In settled weather, which is quite frequent along the South Coast, passages from one harbour to another, or from the Island across to the mainland are quite within the sensible limits of a good dinghy. For the young, these waters are among the finest around the country for learning the important lesson that winds and tides rule everything. Out from the shelter of harbours and creeks the Solent is not to be trifled with. The strength of its tides is often a surprise to visitors, and especially to the racers aboard visiting yachts. Those tides running against a moderate breeze can raise a steep sea, familiarly known as the 'Solent lop' but which, in a craft too small or too flimsy for the job, can be quite daunting. Generally, though, the Solent's delights favour small craft. For the young, cutting their cruising teeth in a dinghy, in which a canvas cover can be slung from the boom to provide rough but comfortable overnight quarters, these waters are perfect.

More harbours charge dues to visitors these days, though Harbourmasters around the Solent might look with indulgence on a small camping dinghy seeking a quiet backwater for a night's stay and waive any fee for a craft which demands nothing in the way of facilities. Even so, it is always wise, as well as courteous, to hail the Harbourmaster on arrival and get his advice. It's always worth having, and comforting to know at least one friendly expert eye will be glancing occasionally in your direction.

Always have some small change handy on visiting Newtown. There, everybody pays. But nobody ever asked for money more charmingly than did Mr Bernard Smith, who was the National Trust's man in Newtown for 25 years, from the time they took over administration of the creeks until he retired at the end of 1986. It would only be a short while after a visitor's anchor went down before Bernard's small clinker launch would chug into view. On his retirement he had messages from people from far and near, and enough bottles of sailor's comfort to start a cellar. Launching facilities for small boats around the Solent shores are many, but varied. There are public launching slipways, and some with good car parking nearby, which is a very different matter. The best up-to-date guide to these is a book called *Where to Launch Your Boat*, published by Barnacle Marine at Colchester. A copy of this, together with the two Ordnance Survey large-scale Outdoor Leisure maps of the Isle of Wight and the New Forest, will be as useful to small-boat explorers as is the indispensable Adlard Coles *Creeks and Harbours of the Solent*, which should be among every cruising skipper's gear.

At present there is no central authority which controls the Solent or its navigable waterways. Harbours can be administered by various authorities: the Queen's Harbourmaster for the Portsmouth area, the National Trust at Newtown, the Beaulieu Estates office for the Beaulieu

River, or the Harbour Commissioners on behalf of the relevant local councils as at Cowes or Yarmouth. Despite this diversity most byelaws are a matter of common sense which can be reduced to a few essentials applicable to all: speed limits in harbour entrances and mooring areas, for example, the dumping of rubbish, landing on foreshores dedicated as nature reserves, or water skiing where it could cause nuisance and danger to other water users including swimmers.

Over the years since the sailing boom of the mid-1950s, the increasing leisure pressures on the Solent have been assessed with varying degrees of concern. The number of craft now moored within the Solent area is now awesomely high. Fortunately, only a proportion of them are on the move at any one time. The coming of marinas, at one time greeted with suspicion by old-time sailors, are now seen increasingly as easing the pressure on rivers which were in danger of being lined with moorings almost without a break for their navigable length. What's more, marinas offer a chance to get rid of shipboard rubbish easily instead of committing it to the river. Sadly, there are still many people who think that the wide waters of the Solent make a commodious place to dump things. If they must chuck their beer and cola cans into the sea, they should at least spike a hole in the bottom end. There is no excuse for discarding plastic of any sort: bottles and polythene are washed ashore in hideous quantities along the Solent's lee shores, especially from the mouth of the Hamble at Warsash along to Stokes Bay. Some of this might be blamed on ferry passengers or, more probably, on the cheerful 'chuck it' attitude which seems so widespread among the crews of large merchant vessels. But if people are content to litter city streets in full view of everybody, what hope for the Solent where it is so easy to do it unobserved?

Thirty years ago the Society for the Protection of the Solent Area was formed, as the result of a call to arms led by the magazine *Yachting World* and its then editor, the doughty E. F. Haylock, to unite opposition to the siting of an oil refinery at Hook on the east side of Southampton Water opposite Calshot. Since that time, during which it has changed its title to the Solent Protection Society, it has used the weapons of quiet consulta-tion and vigilance. It may not be a yapping watchdog, but it is an effective watchdog none the less and its voice, when matters concerning all users of the Solent are raised, is one that local authorities and industrialists listen to.

The Society is not a band of anti-industry yachtsmen. It seeks to safeguard the Solent for everybody, naturalists and walkers as well as sailors, based on its creed which has barely changed since the battle over Hook Refinery: namely, that the Solent is too precious an amenity, within easy reach of millions of people enjoying increased leisure, to be spoiled by piecemeal developments or ill-planned nibbles at its fair countryside.

The concept of administering the Solent as a National Waterpark, with similar status to National Parks inland, has much to commend it, and there would be much for an overall authority to keep under observation. Maximum tolerable moorings on rivers, for example: or oil drilling in the New Forest and its effects on the Solent; or the possible effects on shorelines of gravel extraction on the Solent Banks. Whether or not the Solent as we know it now 'just happened', it is certain that its ruin could come about the same way if those who live beside it and those who visit it or earn their living from it pursue their own interest without considering the greatest good for the greatest number.

The chance to enjoy what is left of its unspoiled land and seascape is a precious balm in an overcrowded and overfenced world. The Solent still has some of the remoteness and peace of the East Coast estuaries, and some of the wooded riverside scenery of the West Country. As more people are attracted to better their fortunes in the South, the place needs all the sensible and unobtrusive management it can get.

Bibliography

Alker Tripp, H. *The Solent and Southern Waters* (1928; reprinted by Conway Maritime Press, 1973)

Bruce, Peter *Solent Hazards* (Boldre Marine, 1985)

Colebourne, Phil *Hampshire's Countryside Heritage: 7, The Coast* (Hampshire County Council, 1984)

Coles, Adlard and Sylvester-Bradley, David *Creeks and Harbours of the Solent* (Nautical Publishing, 1987)

Cowper, Frank *Sailing Tours Part II: The Nore to the Scilly Isles* (1892; facsimile reprint by Ashford Press, 1985)

Dear, Ian *The Royal Yacht Squadron* (Stanley Paul, 1985)

Drummond, Maldwin *The Riddle* (Nautical Books, 1985)

Goss, James *Portsmouth-built Warships 1497–1967* (Kenneth Mason, 1984)

Holland, A. K. *Buckler's Hard: A Rural Shipbuilding Centre* (Kenneth Mason, 1985)

Jowitt, R. L. P. and Jowitt, Dorothy M. *The Solent and its Surroundings* (Terence Dalton, 1978)

Mitchell, Garry et al *Spit Bank and the Spithead Forts* (G. H. Mitchell, 1986)

Morley, Geoffrey *Smuggling in Hampshire and Dorset 1700–1850* (Countryside Books, 1983)

O'Brien, Captain F. T. *Early Solent Steamers* (David & Charles, 1967)

Pannell, J. P. M. *Old Southampton Shores* (David and Charles, 1967)

The Portsmouth Guidebook (Milestone Publications, 1984)

Scott Hughes, John *Harbours of the Solent* (Christopher Johnson, 1956)

Shurlock, Barry *Portrait of the Solent* (Robert Hale, 1983)

Index